*Management
for Your
Church*

Management for Your Church

Alvin J. Lindgren
Norman Shawchuck

ABINGDON
Nashville

MANAGEMENT FOR YOUR CHURCH:
A SYSTEMS APPROACH

Copyright © 1977 by Abingdon

Library of Congress Cataloging in Publication Data

LINDGREN, ALVIN J
  Management for your church.
  Bibliography: p.
  Includes index.
  1. Church management. I. Shawchuck, Norman,
1935-   joint author. II. Title.
BV652.L57   254   77-425

ISBN 0-687-23062-4

MANUFACTURED BY THE PARTHENON PRESS AT
NASHVILLE, TENNESSEE, UNITED STATES OF AMERICA

Contents

Management for Your Church

Preface

This is a book on the theory and management of a
church organization—a practical theology for the church
seeking to be missionally effective in its ministry to a
turbulent environment. As such, the book deals with the
issue of effecting those kinds of church organizational
structures through which God and persons can best work
together.

We intend this book to build upon my earlier volume,
Foundations for Purposeful Church Administration. That volume gives a comprehensive philosophy of the nature and
function of church administration as a dynamic process
through which the church moves to fulfill its purpose. As the
title suggests, it is a foundation volume identifying basic
assumptions, principles, and processes.

This volume builds a systems church management structure upon those foundations. Church management is looked
at within the total context of the practice of ministry, and
systems theory is explored within the context of other
organizational theories. Careful attention is then given to

7

understanding the systems theory of organizations by using the local church as illustrative. The authors seek to offer concrete help to readers by sharing several systems "tools" they have found helpful in working with local churches. These include involving a congregation in identifying its mission, developing an approach for relating to environment, undertaking a specific program for building a program-planning and budgeting system (PPBS), and instituting a method of problem-solving. Finally, we have personalized the systems management concepts by identifying what is involved when the pastor decides to assume the role of church manager.

We are grateful to all who have helped us sharpen the concepts presented here. These persons were members of seminary classes, local churches where the writers have served as consultants, and training groups where we have served as leaders. The critical, responsive, and encouraging responses have added much to whatever wisdom and help is contained here.

We want to say thanks to Mary Ann Mueller, who was our silent partner (and many times not so silent) in preparing this manuscript. She designed the charts and models, deciphered our writing in order to reduce our scribbles to neat rows of typing, and supported and prodded us along the way. We couldn't have had a better colleague in this venture.

Finally, to our families, who allowed us time for research, writing, and rewriting, we express sincere gratitude and love.

It is our hope that this volume will stimulate pastors and laity to utilize the various approaches suggested so that local churches, and the persons in them, may be renewed and come alive.

Alvin J. Lindgren

Glossary

Since we decided to aim our writing toward readers of many denominations, one of the first problems we confronted was that of choosing terms that would clearly communicate across denominational lines. Our approach has been to attempt establishing neutral terms that each reader can apply to the terms commonly used by his or her denomination.

Following is a list of terms often used in the text, with the definitions we wish the reader to assume:

1. *Administrative board:* The governing body of a local church comprised of clergy and lay members—e.g., Parish Council, Catholic Church; Administrative Board, The United Methodist Church; Session, the United Presbyterian Church. Generally the principles discussed relative to an administrative board apply to all decision-making bodies of the church; school boards, councils on ministry, elders, etc.

2. *Church:* When spelled with a capital C, refers to church in general or to a denomination. When spelled with a lower case c, refers to a local body of believers in a given

location—e.g., parish, Catholic Church; charge or larger parish, The United Methodist Church; The United Presbyterian Church.

3. *Clergy:* Persons officially and sacramentally set apart to engage in professional ministry—*e.g.,* pastors, priests, sisters, etc.

4. *Goal:* A desired state or accomplishment.
   Objectives: Concrete, specific, measurable steps toward reaching a goal.
   Criteria: Units of measurement to determine the degree to which an objective is reached.

5. *Management:* The function of providing spiritual and organizational leadership to the church or the area of the church for which the person is responsible. It involves the work of the clergy and lay officials, including all functions of enabling the church to establish its mission and facilitate movement toward it.

6. *Manager:* A clergy or lay official who is responsible for offering spiritual and organizational leadership to a given area of the church—*e.g.,* pastor, parish staff, volunteer lay officers, deacons, ecclesiastical officials.

7. *Systems:* An abbreviated form of organizational systems theory.

8. *Tradition:* Refers to the accepted experience and wisdom of the Church through the centuries.

Introduction

ON WORMS AND CHURCHES

Throughout this book we will use organizational systems theory to help us conceptualize the components of a local church and to discover ways of effecting desired changes in the components.

As a small boy I spent many hours with my father sitting on the banks of a river with nothing between us but a can of worms. Time after time, I used to view the worms with amazement. It always seemed, no matter how large the can, that they always would be found at the bottom, a tight, confused ball of wiggling, squirming worm-flesh. The ball seemed to be moving in every direction, but it really never went anywhere. I could never tell where one worm began and another ended, and when I reached in to grab one, the whole ball would react as though I had touched every one of them.

Often in my haste I would grab one and pull, only to wind up with a torn end of the worm, too small to use; and always my Dad would tell me I shouldn't jerk a worm out of the ball, but that I should take a firm grip on one and apply a steady pull, allowing the worm time to work itself free from the rest.

A local church is very much like a can of worms. The church is the can (system); and every department, function, committee, program, constituency, and so on, is a worm (subsystem). All the subsystems are moving in their own directions, doing their own things; and yet they are always entangled, overlapping, unable to move very far in one direction or to accomplish very much without similar movement in all the other subsystems.

It is, then, no surprise that the prospect of implementing a change is often viewed by many as opening a can of worms that perhaps is better left unopened.

The systems approach is an attempt to identify all those worms before the can is opened, to get them untangled and laid out side by side in order that the structure and function of each may be analyzed. Such a systems approach to a local church will provide the tools to realize the following expectations and desired outcomes:

1. To bring a clear grasp of how a church can utilize systems theory in moving toward its mission.
2. To relate selected aspects of systems theory to the local church and its subsystems by setting forth specific design models and processes applicable to church settings.
3. To introduce clergy and laity to resources, processes, and techniques that may enhance their individual leadership effectiveness. It is expected that the reader will be motivated to pursue additional resources in the field through reading, training events, experimenting in the parish, and the use of consultants.

The purpose of this book is to enlarge the resources of clergy and laity who have administrative leadership responsibilities in the local church and who are willing to explore the viability of the insights of systems concepts applied to the church.

Norman Shawchuck

CHAPTER 1
A Balanced Ministry for Today's Church

Come with me, and I will make you fishers of men.

Matthew 4:18 NEB

Why a book on the theory and management of church organizations? Why should you take time to read it? We shall attempt to answer these questions in this chapter. Perhaps a good place to begin is with a story.

Once upon a time an old man purchased a long neglected piece of property. It was rough and ugly, littered with weeds and thorns. On the property was a tiny rock house—broken, sagging, cracking, leaking. The old man worked on the property for five hard, long years, and under his loving care it became a showplace. The garden was magnificent. The tiny house was cheery and inviting. People visited to relax in the garden, enjoy the sparkling pools, gaze upon the beautiful flowerbeds, and rest for a while in the comfort of the little house. One day a friend who hadn't seen the old man in many years came by for a visit. He walked around the property absolutely enthralled. "This is beautiful! Absolutely magnificent! Simply fantastic! Isn't it marvelous to view the handiwork of God?" "Humph!" snorted the old man. "You should have seen it when God worked it alone."

There is a similarity between the need for gardeners skilled in the art of arranging and tending plants to maintain beautiful gardens, and the need for pastors skilled in the art of building and managing effective organizations to develop God's handiwork.

Christ came into the world with a mission: "It is meat and drink for me to do the will of him who sent me" (John 4:34 NEB). And when he left the world he charged the Church with this same great mission: "Go forth therefore and make all nations my disciples; baptize men everywhere in the name of the Father and the Son and the Holy Spirit, and teach them to observe all that I have commanded you" (Matt. 28:19-20 NEB). This may be called the great co-mission because it is his and ours, and when the Church is engaged in this mission she has the promise of his presence: "And be assured, I am with you always, to the end of time" (Matt. 28:20 NEB).

Christ's spirit is moving in the world, but the success of this co-mission depends upon his best effort and ours.He told us the *what* but depends on us to provide the *how*. He has declared the purpose, but leaves it to us to provide the organization and the plans; and if we leave untapped the tremendous amount of learning that is available to us regarding organization theory and management, we hurt his chances. God could do it alone, but apparently he won't.

This is not too surprising, however, for he has usually chosen to share his purposes with those who believe in him—to share in such a way that he and they share in the successes and failures of the effort. God has chosen us as his co-workers. And it is almost a truism that, having established a relationship with us, he leaves us at liberty to plan and organize our work according to our best judgments.

God has always chosen to work through persons in the actual carrying out of his will. When God purposed to redeem the Israelites from Egyptian bondage, he chose to do so as a co-mission with Moses. So, after some degree of bargaining, they arrived at a contract: God would deal with Pharaoh, and Moses would lead the people out (Exod. 3–4). Moses chose to manage the affairs of the congregation as a one-man show, a decision that almost did him in and the congregation too. It was old Jethro, however, and not God, who finally suggested to him a more effective style of management and organizational structure (Exod. 18:13-27).

When God purposed to ensure that life would continue through the flood, he chose to do so as a co-mission with Noah. God told Noah *what* (build an ark), but left it up to Noah to figure out *how* (Gen. 6:9-21). No wonder it took Noah so long to build the ark.[1] No one had ever built an ark before. Blueprints and how-to-do-it guides for amateur ark builders were hard to come by. He was forced to learn his ark-building by trial and error; yet we have no record of God offering any procedural instructions. God certainly could have offered some good advice: "Now, Noah, hold that plank up there, take a twenty-penny nail and . . ." He could have given that kind of advice, but apparently he didn't.

Throughout all human history God has chosen to carry out his redemptive mission in a working relationship with his chosen persons. Those who join him in this mission take on a responsibility of sufficient importance to God that he is willing to rest the success or failure of the mission, to a large degree, upon the skills, knowledge, and commitment of his chosen persons.

Christians are aware of their working relationship with God and of the awesome extent to which God rests the success of his redemptive mission upon their abilities. For this reason, pastors and other church leaders in America are presently enrolling in continuing-education workshops and post-seminary degree programs in record numbers. But to renew ourselves in scripture, theology, liturgy, and so forth, and not attend to what kinds of organizational structures and management procedures are most effective in our modern environment, is, it seems to us, only to renew ourselves halfway and to expose ourselves to the risk of utter disillusionment when all the thinking in liturgy, scripture, and theology is frustrated by organizational structures and leadership styles that do not serve, but rather inhibit, all that renewed thought and spirit. We do not care to press this claim for all types of ministry. Clearly there are those which depend little upon such skills on the part of the minister. For the pastor, however, skills and knowledge about organization design and management are a growing necessity.

Every pastor recognizes as part of his or her responsibility the need to provide all members of the church opportunities for:

1. Spiritual growth and renewal.
2. Service and stewardship of one's resources before God.
3. Ministering to the spiritual, social, and physical needs of persons in the community and around the world.

All efforts to provide these opportunities, in order to be effective, require organizational structure and programming. In any church the achievement of the individual member's personal goals and interests is heavily dependent upon the ability of the pastor to provide the kind of organizational structures, polity, and climate that are conducive to the personal and spiritual growth of its members. A pastor, then, in order to provide a balanced ministry to the congregation, must be as skillful in designing and managing effective organizations as he or she is in preaching, theologizing, and counseling.

Perhaps few persons in America have given more thought to church organizational theory than has Robert Worley, of McCormick Theological Seminary, Chicago.[2] In a paper he delivered on this subject, Dr. Worley said:

The identification of the need for knowledge about church organizations and leadership of these organizations is embarrassing, or it ought to be embarrassing. We . . . need only to look again at Calvin's description of the office which was assigned Christ to recognize the source of embarrassment. The office, as Calvin suggested, consisted of three parts, prophetic, priestly, and kingly.[3] Calvin maintained the three activities by the One who occupied the office were necessary for our knowledge of God's work in Christ, and the receiving of the benefits of this work by us. It is important to emphasize that prophetic, priestly and kingly activities were essential in the witness, the sharing, the expression of God's work in Christ.

It is, however, strongly characteristic of Protestantism that the prophetic-preaching and the sacramental-pastoral roles have been emphasized while the kingly (organizational), governance or wise-rule (management) activity has been largely neglected.

I am suggesting that the crises of clergy are related to the turbulence in church organizations and that we must now focus on the organizations and the functions of governance in these organizations as at least a partial answer to these crises. There is a theological basis for this focus as well as an organizational and social-psychological basis. Calvin saw the *three* activities as necessary and essential expressions of God's work in Christ. All three belong together, expressing their own aspect of that work in unity with one another. It is possible for the three activities to contradict each other. The lack of a unified understanding of Christ's ministry and its implications for our ministry has both theological and practical consequences for the church professional and the church organization.

My argument can be summarized. We must understand church organizations in their uniqueness as church organizations and in their commonness with other organizations, and we must provide leadership for contemporary church organizations. Wise rule is one of those essential activities along with prophetic and priestly activities which helps to shape the witness of Christ's people to God's work among them, and is itself a witness to that work. Governance is an activity which is practical, concrete and a profound expression of theological reflection.[4]

Calvin conceived of the pastor's role as involving these three functions: prophetic, priestly, and kingly. For Calvin these functions were of equal importance to the life and well-being of the church and were necessary to provide a balanced ministry. Briefly the functions involve:

Prophetic—Calling the church to human love and justice; challenging, discomforting, warning. Most clearly seen in the activity of preaching.

Priestly—Calling the church to its highest possible spiritual state; consoling, comforting, accepting, forgiving. Most clearly seen in pastoral-sacramental activities (administering sacraments, counseling, and so forth).

Kingly—Administering wisely and effectively the re-

17

sources God has given the church. Most clearly seen in organizational activities (management, planning, training, and so on).

The practice of ministry to which God calls the pastor involves ministry to the organization as well as to individuals. Any pastor who views management and organizational responsibilities as a necessary evil is threatened with an unbalanced ministry. Any pastor who prepares and renews himself or herself in the areas of the prophetic and priestly functions of ministry, and neglects preparation and renewal in the organizational functions, will not offer a balanced ministry to the church.

The kingly function of the pastor's role is a ministry to the organizational structures and processes of the church. The pastor should no more be willing to abdicate this ministry than he or she would the prophetic or priestly ministry. Indeed, since many of the personal goals, needs, and interests of individuals in the church can be met only through organized programs and group activity, it becomes apparent that one way a pastor can minister to human beings is to minister effectively to the organizational aspects of the church.

Working with God to achieve his mission and ours in a local church has always been a serious and complex matter. This task, however, is now much complicated by changes in the environment, which demand more changes in the organizational structures and polity of the church than ever before. These necessary changes issue a call to pastors everywhere for more study in organizational theory and management. Plato used to tell a story relative to the tremendous need for us to learn in all these areas. In his *Republic* he says: "Suppose this to be the situation on board a ship. The captain is stronger than any of the crew, but he is a little bit hard of hearing and a little bit short-sighted. And while he knows a little about navigation, he doesn't know very much about it. The crew, on the other hand, doesn't know anything about navigation. However, they spend all their time quarreling with one another about how the ship ought to be run, each of them contending that he ought to be at the helm. They devote their greatest admiration to the man who can, by force or fraud, manipulate the captain. The crew has no idea that properly navigating a ship requires knowledge of the seasons of the year, the sky, the stars, the wind, the tide. In fact, the crew feels you don't have to know anything—just get the helm. There is no such thing as the professional study of navigation. There is no such thing as an art of navigation or a science of navigation. And if someone were to come on board and attempt to tell the crew, 'You are not ready to take over the helm because you have not yet studied the seasons, stars, the wind, and the tide,' they would throw him overboard as a stargazer, an idle gossiper, a philosopher—someone secretly trying to cheat the captain." The point of this delightful story is not that the deaf, short-sighted captain doesn't know very much. As a matter of fact, he is almost the hero because he knows so much more than anybody else on the crew. The point of the story is that the crew members, all clammering for the helm, are not yet fit for the helm, and that tremendous study, learning, and knowledge are necessary to prepare one for the helm. The crew, however, is not at all aware of this, because much of that study is of subjects apparently not related to navigating a ship. And so too, in respect to leading a local church, we have a lot of stars, tides, and winds to study in order to navigate more effectively and sail a little bit better. Much of this study seems remote because we have been conditioned to emphasize the priestly and prophetic functions of pastoral leadership. Nonetheless, the kingly function is necessary to navigating the church, and, like the wind, seasons, stars, and tides, there are organizational and management areas we need to study. We need to do ever more studying in these areas, to learn more, and to put our knowledge to work. God's great mission, and ours, will be better because of it.

> *Study to show thyself approved unto God, a*
> *workman that needeth not to be ashamed.*
> II Timothy 2:15 KJV

CHAPTER 2

The Influence
of Organization Theory
on the Practice
of Ministry

*And we will appoint them to deal with these
matters, while we devote ourselves to prayer
and the ministry of the Word.*
Acts 6:3, 4 NEB

There are many organizational theories. In the
next few pages we will introduce you to five that are
operative in the Church today. These are theories of how an
organization should be structured and managed, how people
should relate to one another within the organization, and
what constitutes appropriate leadership behavior. A consideration of such issues seems a prerequisite to any conscious
attempt to learn how to become a better leader of church
organizations. *Conscious* is the key word here because many
church leaders carry out their organizational responsibilities
more or less intuitively. Some are very gifted leaders, and
wherever they go the church "gets its act together" and
moves forward into mission and ministry. Those of us who
are not so gifted need to think through our own organizational concepts and behaviors, and explore the range of
organizational theories and styles available to us.

All church leaders have opinions and preferences about
how their organization should be structured and managed.
Many, however, who are not pleased with the results of their
leadership are not conscious of the influence their opinions

and preferences have upon their effectiveness, or lack of it, in the church. Again *conscious* is the key word, because many of us have never taken time to think through our own ideas, which remain vague and foggy notions, unarticulated opinions operating at an unconscious level within us. But as vague and foggy, as unarticulated and unconscious as they may be, they nonetheless act as powerful motivators influencing the way we organize our church, the styles of leadership we use,[1] the way we relate to the members of the church, and the way we expect them to relate to us.

The ideas you hold, consciously or unconsciously, regarding appropriate organizational design and leadership behavior constitute what might be called your *preferred theory of church organization*. It seems logical to us that you should know what your theory is and what the real life implications of that theory, put into practice, will most likely be for your church.

ORGANIZATION THEORIES IN PRACTICE

As we said earlier, there are many organizational theories, five of which we shall briefly discuss in this chapter: traditional, charismatic, human relations, classical (bureaucratic), and systems. We have chosen these from among many, because they should serve quite well to introduce some components of organizational theories and to give a feel for the influence each theory might have upon a church organization when it is espoused by the leaders and put into practice.

The Traditional Theory

The traditional theory focuses on the need to maintain the tradition by preserving the *status quo*. This theory views the leader's main function to be that of transmitting the heritage and of participating in ceremonial affairs. It sees the organization as a static, patrimonial institution whose primary concern is to safeguard the people from change, which is always seen as a threat to the tradition. In this

21

theory, members of the organization are expected to have little initiative, no desire for progress, and little creativity, because internal threat to the *status quo* is even more disconcerting than external threat.

Perhaps no denomination or confession in America has espoused the traditional theory as the most appropriate organizational model for its agencies and churches. We all, however, have experienced elements of this theory in various churches and church groups. Possibly we all know some church leaders whose leadership style would seem to indicate that they espouse, consciously or unconsciously, the traditional theory.

The Charismatic Leader Theory

The charismatic leader theory focuses on an intuition, a vision, or a call. It is the leader's main function to interpret and proclaim this message and to inspire the people to join together in rejecting the *status quo* and pursuing the organization's mission. The theory views persons in the organization as active and capable of rendering valuable service, but always in need of aggressive, directive leadership.

The charismatic leader theory is more common than the traditional in the American religious community. Some well-known examples of this theory in practice are the Billy Graham Evangelistic Association, the Oral Roberts Association, and Martin Luther King's leadership of the civil rights movement.[2]

The Human Relations Theory

The human relations theory focuses on the need for persons to experience personal growth and to achieve their own personal goals in the organization. Human relations sees the organization as a servant of the people, a means by which persons can experience self-worth, expression, and personal goal achievement. The leader's main function is to create an atmosphere conducive to open expression and democratic participation for all persons.

Some examples of religious organizations based upon human relations theory are the Unitarian-Universalist Association and the Ethical Humanist Society. The greatest influence of human relations theory upon American religious systems, however, is to be seen in units or groups within denominations and local churches focusing attention on feelings, mutual acceptance, and personal goals.

The Classical Theory

The classical theory (more commonly called bureaucratic) focuses on the achievement of organizational goals. In this theory persons are seen as servants of the organization, a means by which the organization can achieve its goals. The theory views the leader's function as that of maintaining control by enforcing the rules and handing down decisions from the top. Two examples of religious organizations based upon the classical theory are The United Methodist Church and the Roman Catholic Church.

The human relations and classical theories are the most practiced organizational theories within the American religious community. Indeed, nearly every denomination or communion is structured along the lines of one or the other of these theories. In addition, there is a great deal of intermingling of these two theories within organizations. For example, the Catholic Church structure is based upon classical organization theory, while the Catholic charismatic movement is using a human relations approach.

The Systems Theory

Our intention here is not to describe systems theory, since that will be the burden of the following chapter, but to show its relationship to the human relations and classical theories and to list some of its contributions to the field of organization theory.

Systems theory is the latest of the five theories discussed in this chapter, dating back to about 1960. It is also perhaps the least known and practiced by American religious organizations. Why, then, should you be interested in it? Are not the older, proved theories more desirable? Perhaps in some instances; but generally, we believe, the systems approach will prove more effective. Most of the positive factors of the other theories are encompassed in systems theory and put into perspective. Let us briefly compare the systems approach to the classical and human relations theories.

The Relationship of Systems to Human-Relations and Classical Theories   The bureaucratic organization focuses on achieving the organization's goals, while the human-relations organization focuses on achieving the goals of its people. Systems theory, however, holds organizational growth and goal achievement, and the growth of persons and the achievement of their own goals within the organization, to be of equal importance.

If an organization is primarily task oriented, a bureaucratic style will prove most effective. If an organization is primarily person oriented, a human-relations style will prove most effective. If, however, the organization understands persons to need organizations and structure in order to achieve many of their personal goals, and if it understands itself to need persons in order to achieve its organizational goals, a systems approach will prove most effective, since systems theory holds the organizational goals and the goals of persons to be of equal importance. Systems theory addresses the interrelatedness and interdependency of the organization and its people.

We cannot yet identify any denomination or communion based primarily upon systems theory. This, however, is not because systems theory is inappropriate or ineffective, but because it is a much later and less familiar organizational design.

Systems theory was developed as an attempt on the part of organizations to cope with rapidly changing environmental conditions. All indications are that rapid and radical environmental change will remain a fact of life for our churches. We feel quite confident, therefore, in predicting that systems theory is here to stay, and religious systems in the future will take on more of the systems approach both in order to survive and in order to achieve their mission in a constantly changing environment.

Systems Theory's Contributions to the Field of Organizational Theory   Systems theory is a more satisfactory approach to organizational effectiveness in the midst of rapid and radical environmental change. We will attempt to explain this increased effectiveness by listing some of this theory's unique contributions to organizational theory.

1. The systems approach offers diagnostic tools for identifying problems, and helps to get a handle on the dynamics that cause the church to behave as it does.
2. A systems view will greatly increase the effectiveness of any planning process by identifying all the components of the church and its environment that will act as resources or constraints upon the plan.
3. Systems thinking offers a perspective of wholeness, a gestaltview of the entire church that is often easily overlooked because of one's involvement in a particular organization within the church.
4. The systems approach enables a leader or group to predict more accurately the effects and implications of alternative courses of action.
5. A systems view keeps the church from being totally focused in upon itself by requiring it to see itself in relationship with other systems in its environment.
6. Systems theory elicits flexible leadership behavior contingent upon conditions in the environment, the goals, and characteristics of the church.

Characteristics of Various Organizational Theories

Earlier in this chapter, we said each leader holds a "set" of opinions about how the Church should be structured and managed. This set of opinions, we said, constitutes the leader's organizational theory. Following is a matrix of several organizational components about which opinions may be held as they tend to cluster in each of the five theories we have discussed.[3]

ORGANIZATIONAL
ORGANIZATIONAL
THEORIES

THEORY: and Symbol	DESCRIPTIVE ORGANIZATIONAL AND THEOLOGICAL TERMS	CONCEPT OF ORGANIZATION	DECISION-MAKING PROCESS	LEADER'S FUNCTIONS AND STYLE
TRADITIONAL	*Organizational:* Patrimonial *Theological:* "The People of God"	Maintaining a tradition.	Made and announced by the elders. Unhurried pace.	To maintain the tradition and preserve the status quo. PATERNAL PRIESTLY
CHARISMATIC	*Organizational:* Intuitive *Theological:* "The new creation"	Pursuing an intuition.	Spontaneous, unpredictable proclamation by leader.	To lead and motivate through personal appeal. PROPHETIC INSPIRATIONAL
CLASSICAL	*Organizational:* Bureaucratic *Theological:* "God's Building"	Running a machine.	Issuance of orders from the top; conscious, rationalized, calculated.	To direct by handing down decisions. AGGRESSIVE DIRECTIVE
HUMAN RELATIONS	*Organizational:* Group or democratic *Theological:* "The Fellowship of Faith"	Leading groups.	Group decision through informal, intimate, and fluid relationships.	To create an atmosphere conducive to expression and participation. SENSITIVE NON-DIRECTIVE
SYSTEMS Input → Transformation → Output	*Organizational:* Organic *Theological:* "The Body of Christ"	Adapting a system.	Continuous adaptation with purpose kept relevant to environment.	To clarify goals, interpret environment, and monitor change. PROFESSIONAL ACTIVATOR

In reviewing the matrix it is important to keep in mind that there are no pure examples of any of the theories in actual practice. Each denomination and local church will possess elements of most, if not all, of the theories. However, each denomination or local church tends to be predominantly influenced by one of the theories, so that it might be said to have a preferred organizational theory with elements of the others.[4]

We encourage you to take a few minutes to identify your preferred organizational theory and any elements of the

COMPONENTS

STYLES OF CONFLICT MANAGEMENT	RELATIONSHIP TO ENVIRONMENT	VIEW OF "PERSONS"	COMMUNICATION PATTERN	GOALS
Rejecting and ignoring forces which threaten stability or the status quo.	Rejection of external change to maintain status quo.	Persons are secure in the status quo; little initiative is expected.	Leader transmits heritage, expecting unexplicit consent.	Generally assumed and seldom articulated.
Welcoming challenge; thriving on conflict.	Rejection of the status quo; articulation of changes.	Persons are active and capable, but need constant direction and intervention.	Leader announces the content of intuition; he and his followers are bound to obey.	Highly explicit, reflecting the philosophy and aims of the leader.
Bringing about subjection to authority through directives and appeal to written policy.	Resolution of tension with environment by domination or cooptation.	Persons need controls and prefer direction.	Leader issues detailed directives; most communication is downward from the top.	Objective and quantitative; arrived at by hierarchy and handed down.
Resolving conflict through compromise.	Respect for and fluid relationships with the environment.	Persons learn to seek and accept responsibility when properly motivated.	Leader encourages individual participation and contribution; the group shares.	Subjective rather than objective; purposes of the group emerge from discussion.
Integrating creative elements of conflict to achieve benefit therefrom.	Attuned to changing environment; adaptive, flexible relationships.	Not all have same skills & knowledge. Can be motivated through goal clarification enablement and effectiveness.	In all directions, through open channels and "linking" persons.	Definitive and unifying, with consideration for environment.

others you are attempting to put into practice in your ministry. You can do this by returning to the chart to conduct a self-analysis as follows:

1. Place a card over the three left-hand columns, which deal with theoretical issues.
2. Read *down* each of the seven columns of Organizational Components, and encircle the one statement in each column that is most descriptive of your own preferences regarding that particular component.
3. Remove the card to see which organizational theory you

have most often encircled, giving you some indication of your present preferences.

The value of the exercise will depend upon your willingness to encircle the statement in each component column that most nearly describes your preferences as they really are, not the statements that you believe the authors, or someone else, would want you to encircle.

We have briefly introduced you to five organizational theories and have attempted to show that each theory views the components of the organization from a different perspective. We shall now turn our attention to systems theory, discussing the theory from the viewpoint of a system's components, and the implications of the theory upon one's practice of ministry.

> *Unless the Lord builds the house,*
> *its builders will have toiled in vain.*
> Psalm 127:1 NEB

CHAPTER 3
Viewing the Church From a Systems Perspective

God shall supply all you need according to his
riches in glory by Christ Jesus.
Philippians 4:19 KJV

PROBLEMS VS. CAUSES

The Community Church administrative board, which welcomed the district superintendent to the special meeting, was a worried group indeed, and it didn't take them long to get directly to the point. "We ended last year with a budget deficit. Now we have just completed our pledge campaign, and the pledges are far too low to carry us through this year. If we don't raise more money, we will simply have to close the doors!"

After some discussion, the district superintendent said, "I think I understand your financial situation. Tell me, what do you hope I might do to help?"

"Help us put together a finance drive that will get us adequate finances to operate our church through the year."

"I can try to do that, but should we not also try to identify the cause of the lack of response to your church's financial needs in order that you might try to solve it?"

After a long moment of silence, one board member said, "We are out of money, and we didn't get enough pledge support to bail us out. Let's solve that before we tackle anything else!"

"I know your budget deficit and the poor response constitutes a real problem. But every problem has a cause, and unless you discover and remove the cause the problem will occur again. Now, what do you think the cause of this problem might be?"

"Well, for one thing, we do such a lousy job of trying to raise funds. We have no organization. We never visit the homes. We think we're so broke we can't even mail out the pledge cards. Instead, we put them out on the back table and ask people to pick the card with their name on it. Most of the cards are never even picked up. I can go back there right now and find cards from last year."

"Well, we all know members who don't support this church because of fights and hard feelings that have been here for years. Instead of supporting the church, they say, 'Oh, I'll start supporting the church when so-and-so stops trying to run everything. If he wants to run it, let him pay for it.'"

"You know, my wife and I talked about this before we made our own pledge this year, and we almost didn't pledge anything either. This church has no purpose or mission. We never talk about anything but money to keep the doors open. Maybe we should close the doors and give our money to churches that are doing something."

"Yeah, we better think about it sooner or later. We haven't had any new members in years, but several have died or moved away."

"Why would anybody want to join this church? We haven't painted this building in years. The Sunday school furniture is falling apart. I've said for years we can't expect children to come if we don't get some adequate Sunday school facilities."

"I don't think it's all our fault. Church just isn't as important as it used to be for a lot of people. I know a lot of boys who would rather play little league than go to Sunday school; and a lot of us men never miss lodge, but we miss church. And besides that, our entire community is hurting economically. I suppose our church isn't the only one that's suffering." Sounds all too familiar, doesn't it?

The budget deficit and the poor results of the pledge campaign were problems, sure enough. But what do you think was the cause of their financial problems? Does your church ever focus its attention and energies on solving problems without getting to the cause of the problem? Why do churches do this? Probably because it is not always easy to locate and define the cause. Sometimes one condition causes many problems, while at other times many conditions combine to cause one problem.

A nosebleed is a problem easy to see, and just about everyone knows how to treat one with ice packs. High blood pressure, however, isn't so easy to see, and an ice pack on the forehead is not an effective solution. When high blood pressure is the cause of the nosebleed, an ice pack may stop the bleeding temporarily, but it will not get at the cause. Chances are, the nose will bleed again. Any good doctor knows it's worth the effort to sort out the symptoms (problems) from the illness (cause), because to treat the symptom will certainly not cure the illness; and unless the illness is cured, the symptoms may become more severe in spite of the treatment.

Let's suppose the district superintendent was able to help the people at Community Church put on a "super pledge" campaign. Do you think this would solve their financial problems, make them worse, or forestall a solution? When the district superintendent encouraged the group to search for the cause of their financial problems, they soon identified many issues confronting their church, such as:

1. Poor organization of the pledge campaign.
2. Hard feelings and divisions between members.
3. No purpose or mission.
4. No new members.
5. Inadequate and unattractive facilities.
6. Competition of other clubs and activities.
7. Low economic status of the community.
8. No concern or ministry outside of themselves.

It was then possible for the superintendent to diagram the relationship of all these issues in order to develop a picture of the church, as on page 33.

The board decided the lack of finances was a serious problem that required immediate attention. However, the financial problems of the church would continue, and possibly worsen, until one of the possible causes on the list had been dealt with: no purpose or mission. At that point, they began making plans for:

1. Reducing some of the immediate financial threat. (First aid for temporary relief.)
2. Involving the congregation in deciding the mission of the church and establishing goals to reach the mission. (Not first aid but sustained treatment.)

We have chosen to use this particular church situation to introduce you to systems theory because the diagnosis offered by the administrative board turned out to be systemic, that is, they looked at every important component of the church system. What is startling in this instance is that they identified some serious conditions in every component.

But what is a system, and what are its components? And how can the systems approach be utilized by church leaders? These are the questions we hope to deal with in the following chapters. We will discuss the church from the viewpoint of systems theory, introduce some systems tools that we hope you will use and find helpful, and attempt to put this all together in terms of the important function of pastoral management as an enabling ministry to help the church become more effective in fulfilling its mission and ministry.

SYSTEMS THEORY OF ORGANIZATION

An organizational system[1] is a set of components that work together to accomplish an overall objective, and that possesses a sufficient boundary to distinguish it from its environment.

If you were to ask someone to identify the components of their church, they would typically answer by identifying

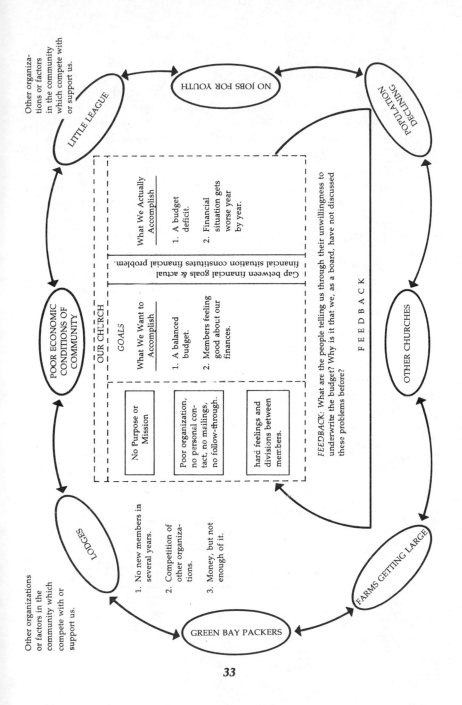

Other organizations or factors in the community which compete with or support us.

LITTLE LEAGUE

NO JOBS FOR YOUTH

POPULATION DECLINING

POOR ECONOMIC CONDITIONS OF COMMUNITY

OUR CHURCH

GOALS

What We Want to Accomplish

1. A balanced budget.
2. Members feeling good about our finances.

No Purpose or Mission

Poor organization, no personal contact, no mailings, no follow-through.

hard feelings and divisions between members.

Gap between financial goals & actual financial situation constitutes financial problem.

What We Actually Accomplish

1. A budget deficit.
2. Financial situation gets worse year by year.

FEEDBACK: What are the people telling us through their unwillingness to underwrite the budget? Why is it that we, as a board, have not discussed these problems before?

F E E D B A C K

OTHER CHURCHES

FARMS GETTING LARGE

GREEN BAY PACKERS

LODGES

1. No new members in several years.
2. Competition of other organizations.
3. Money, but not enough of it.

Other organizations or factors in the community which compete with or support us.

33

organizations, *e.g.*, the Sunday school, women's club, men's club, youth group, official board, choir, trustees. A careful review, however, would indicate each of these organizations, by itself, fits the description of a system that we have given above. Each of these organizations can be distinguished from the other organizations in the church, and each has its own set of components that work together to accomplish an overall purpose. In short, these organizations are subsystems within the church system, and many of them will have subsystems of their own—committees, age-level departments, classes, and so on.

The components that comprise an organizational system are:

1. Input System
2. Transforming System
3. Output System
4. Environment
5. Boundary
6. Feedback Loop

A church, as a system, is comprised of these components,

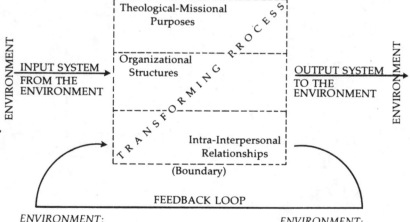

as is each organization (subsystem) within the church. The simple model on page 34 shows the relationship of these components. This model suggests that the transforming process is the heart of the system. Systems theory holds the *transforming process* and the *environment* to be the two components most influential in determining the character of the system. We shall now describe each of the components and discuss its functional relationship to the others.

Input System

The church, like all other systems, in order to survive and carry on its activities must take in raw materials from its environment—new people, money, hired personnel, new technologies and methods, materials, and so on. Churches use various means to obtain these necessary inputs or materials. The every-member canvass is for many churches a major means of bringing in sufficient money to operate the church. Evangelistic crusades, advertising, bus ministries, door-to-door canvassing are all utilized by various churches to bring in sufficient raw materials to carry on the church's ministries. For example, one of the writers first began attending church as a result of a Sunday school contest in which a high school friend was attempting to win a camera. The Sunday school had decided to increase the effectiveness of its input system by offering prizes as a means of inspiring its members to recruit prospects.

The Transforming System

The transforming process[2] of a church is the totality of the means by which the church transforms its raw materials—people, money, technologies, and so forth—into its desired results—conversions, spirituality, social services, trained lay workers. The transforming process comprises three factors that are always in dynamic relationship to one another. These three factors are:

Theological-Missional Purposes   These purposes issue from the theological-biblical beliefs and the values that give a church its unique *identity* and its *reason for being*. They have to do with who the church is and what its ultimate aspirations are. As such, the theological-missional purposes of the church form the core of all areas of its life. (Because of the extreme importance of its theology and missional understanding upon every area of a church's life and being, we have devoted a separate chapter to this aspect of the church, chapter 4.)

Organizational Structures   The church uses organizational structures and processes to accomplish its theological-missional purposes. At issue here are the combinations of human, physical, and spiritual resources the church affects, the political structure and polity of the church, and the processes the church uses to conduct its affairs.

Intra and Interpersonal Relationships   Various levels of human relationships result from the organizational structures and processes that the church creates to accomplish its theological-missional purposes. A church, like any other system, hopes its quality of human relationships will be expressed in such qualities as cooperation, collaboration, enhanced self-image, trust, openness, and so on. However, the church, like all systems, often experiences such relationships as competition, conflict, loss of self-image, alienation.

The Function of the Transforming System   It is the function of the transforming system to receive the raw materials from the input system, to transform and integrate them into a church's programs. The purpose of this function is twofold:

1. To provide energy for the maintenance of the church and its internal programs.
2. To "output" part of the transformed material into the environment in order for the church to influence it.

When a church trains a Sunday school teacher for its own school, it is providing material for itself to maintain its internal programs. But when the church sends one of its teachers as a missionary to another location, it is "outputting" part of its material in order to have an influence on a part of its environment.

When the writer first attended Sunday school with his friend, he came in as raw material. He had never been inside a church building before, had never read a scripture lesson, had no idea what was expected of him or what he could expect of the class. Part of the Sunday school's *input system,* however, was to make him feel welcome and to keep him coming to the school long enough for the school's *transforming system* to begin its work of Christian growth and to integrate him into the system itself. Within a period of several months, the young man became a regular member of the Sunday school class, confessed faith in Christ, was baptized, and became a member of the church. The church's input system had brought him in as raw material, but its transforming system had integrated him to the point where he was now capable of providing energy to help the Sunday school and the church carry on their ministries.

Most materials that come into a church enter in a raw form—that is, they are not fully suited to the church's unique purposes and must be transformed into more suitable material.

It is important to remember that these three aspects—a church's theological-missional purposes, its organizational structures and processes, and its intra-interpersonal relationships—are dynamically interrelated and function interdependently in carrying on the church's transforming process. *And,* because these aspects are interrelated and interdependent, change in any one will affect change in the other two. This concept of dynamic interrelationship and constant change is one of the systems approach's greatest contributions to organization theory.

Output System

A church's output system is composed of the means by which it "exports" a part of its energy and resources (money, people, programs, and such) in order to influence its environment or to support other organizations or causes.

During the writer's senior year of high school, the pastor conversed with him regarding the need for professional ministers in the denomination. In addition, the pastor preached several sermons on the call to ministry, had young guest speakers from denominational schools, and so forth. Thus, after spending some years as a member of the local church, the young man left the community to study in one of the denomination's schools and, upon graduation, to enter the professional ministry. He had become a part of the church's output system.

A Scriptural Basis for Maintaining an Output System

"For if you give, you will get! Your gift will return to you in full and overflowing measure, pressed down, shaken together to make room for more, and running over. Whatever measure you use to give—large or small—will be used to measure what is given back to you" (Luke 6:38 TLB).

All Christians would agree this concept of giving and receiving is a basic principle of Christian theology, and few would disagree that it applies to the church as well as to its members.

It is often difficult, however, for a struggling church to export any of its resources to other organizations while its own maintenance and survival are at stake. Churches, like people, are often tempted to keep all their resources for their own programs. Sooner or later, however, such an attitude will destroy a church, for the measure by which the church gives of its resources to the work of God beyond its own programs and boundaries becomes the measure by which God gives resources (inputs) for its own programs.

To this point, we have discussed the three basic systems components, or areas of activity, in which an organization engages: its input, transforming, and output systems. We shall now turn our attention to three additional components—its environment, boundary, and feedback loop.

Environment

Systems theory views the environment of a system as comprising all other systems (organizational, social, economic, etc.) that influence it, or that the system is seeking to influence. The system exists in a condition of constant interrelatedness and interdependency with other systems in its environment. Any change in the environment calls for an appropriate adaptive response on the part of the system. Perhaps this awareness of the system's dynamic interrelatedness with its environment is the systems approach's greatest contribution to organization theory.[3]

There are, of course, a myriad of systems in the universe, and in your own community, but not all these systems are influencing or being influenced by your church. This fact suggests an important principle that is often overlooked. The environment of your church is to be understood not in terms of geographical proximity, but in terms of the relationship and influence of your church upon other systems, and vice versa. There are perhaps some organizations only a few blocks from your church that are not a part of its environment since there is no relationship or influence between the two. On the other hand, some systems on the other side of the world, or out of this world, may be a part of your church's environment. The Christian belief in heaven suggests at least one system outside of this world that is related to your church and, therefore, a part of its environment.

Earlier in this chapter we said the theological-missional purposes were crucial to the life and being of the church. So also is an adequate understanding of its environment. Thus we have decided to devote a separate chapter to a discussion of the interaction of the church with its environment (see chapter 5).

Boundary
The church exists within an environment of other systems. Its members are also members of many other systems— family, business, school, political party. Yet no one seems to have much difficulty distinguishing the church from these other systems. Some differentiation is made simply upon the basis of physical location and characteristics. These establish the physical boundaries. The major differences between systems, however, are not physical or geographical, but are differences of tradition, beliefs, history, values, and emo-

tions, which establish for each system a totally unique climate, or *sentient boundary*. Decisions that affect the system's boundary are always emotion laden, since they always introduce the risk of altering the identity of the system.

In addition to giving the system its unique identity, the boundary serves to *filter* into its transforming system those raw materials which the system wants and to filter out those materials which it does not want to enter. By the same token, the filtering function serves to keep inside the system those transformed materials which it wishes to use for its own programs and to export those materials which the system wishes to output in order to influence a part of its environment. It needs to be said that there are, at times, certain environmental factors that become so pervasive or overpowering that they affect a church in spite of its every attempt to filter out their influence. For example, television has no doubt affected the life-styles, choices, and values·of persons in every church in the nation, in spite of the concerted efforts many churches made to keep its influence out. This serves to underscore the fact that, for any church, boundary selection is not totally voluntary.

The boundary, then, can best be understood in terms of those characteristics of the system which influence or monitor the transactions and exchanges of the church with its environment. The importance of this monitoring function can hardly be overemphasized. We are all no doubt aware of churches that have filtered in so much of the environment they have lost their unique identity and sense of purpose. On the other hand, there are churches that are so closed as to be out of touch with, and unresponsive to, pressing needs and opportunities for ministry.

The final systems component remaining to be discussed is the feedback loop. We shall now turn our attention to it.

Feedback Loop

A church itself, as well as its environment, is changing even while it is planning and carrying out its ministries. It is to be expected, therefore, that no plan or program will be 100 percent successful. And without constant monitoring and alteration, even the most successful programs and decisions will soon become ineffective. Always expect a gap between the church's desired outputs and its actual outputs—and plan accordingly.

Given that this gap always exists, a church should be constantly gathering information regarding the quantitative and qualitative effects of its ministries and decisions.[4] This information should in turn be used by the church to evaluate its performance in relation to its mission and goals. This is not as difficult as it may appear, since every church is constantly generating information about itself. This feedback information comes in many forms and about many areas of the church's life—staff and membership morale, age and sex statistics of the membership, attendance and financial trends, and the rate of turnover, or lack of it, among volunteer workers, to name a few. A church that does not recognize and utilize its feedback information is denying itself one of its most valuable inputs.

Summary of the Components of a System

We have now identified and described the strategic components of which a church system is comprised. The heart of the church is its *transforming system*. It is here that the church transforms and integrates the materials at its disposal, and consumes the greater portion of its energy and resources to maintain its programs and functions in ministry to its own members.

In order to carry on its transforming functions and to minister to its own members, the church needs materials to work with. Therefore, it consumes a certain amount of its energy and resources in maintaining an *input system*, which is intended to secure sufficient raw materials to ensure its survival and growth.

Even though the church's existence requires it to maintain its own programs and to minister to its own people, it must also attempt to exert a positive influence upon its environment. In order to accomplish this, the church consumes a portion of its energy and resources in maintaining an *output system,* which exports certain resources that the church offers in ministry to people and programs beyond its own boundaries.

Surrounding the church system is its *environment*. Changes in the environment call for changes in the church, if it is to remain relevant and effective.

The church is located within its environment, but it possesses a sufficient *boundary* to differentiate it from all other systems. This boundary, comprising physical and sentient components, can best be understood in terms of the monitoring functions that determine its transactions and exchanges with its environment.

In many ways the church produces information that can be **used to inform itself of the quantitative and qualitative**

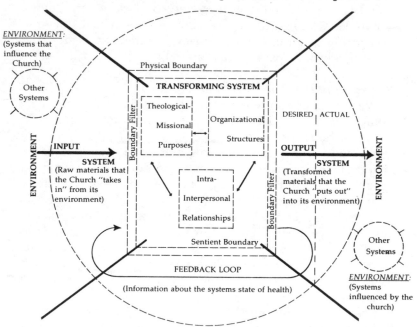

A SYSTEMS DIAGRAM OF AN ORGANIZATION

42

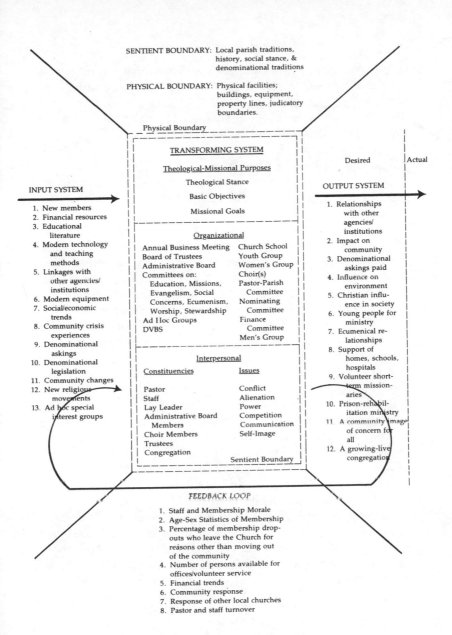

SENTIENT BOUNDARY: Local parish traditions,
history, social stance, &
denominational traditions

PHYSICAL BOUNDARY: Physical facilities;
buildings, equipment,
property lines, judicatory
boundaries.

Physical Boundary

TRANSFORMING SYSTEM

Theological-Missional Purposes

Theological Stance

Basic Objectives

Missional Goals

Desired | Actual

INPUT SYSTEM

1. New members
2. Financial resources
3. Educational
   literature
4. Modern technology
   and teaching
   methods
5. Linkages with
   other agencies/
   institutions
6. Modern equipment
7. Social/economic
   trends
8. Community crisis
   experiences
9. Denominational
   askings
10. Denominational
    legislation
11. Community changes
12. New religious
    movements
13. Ad hoc special
    interest groups

Organizational

Annual Business Meeting   Church School
Board of Trustees   Youth Group
Administrative Board   Women's Group
Committees on: Choir(s)
  Education, Missions,   Pastor-Parish
  Evangelism, Social   Committee
  Concerns, Ecumenism,   Nominating
  Worship, Stewardship   Committee
Ad Hoc Groups   Finance
DVBS   Committee
                          Men's Group

Interpersonal

Constituencies   Issues

Pastor   Conflict
Staff   Alienation
Lay Leader   Power
Administrative Board Competition
  Members   Communication
Choir Members   Self-Image
Trustees
Congregation
                      Sentient Boundary

OUTPUT SYSTEM

1. Relationships
   with other
   agencies/
   institutions
2. Impact on
   community
3. Denominational
   askings paid
4. Influence on
   environment
5. Christian influ-
   ence in society
6. Young people for
   ministry
7. Ecumenical re-
   lationships
8. Support of
   homes, schools,
   hospitals
9. Volunteer short-
   term mission-
   aries
10. Prison-rehabil-
    itation ministry
11. A community image
    of concern for
    all
12. A growing-live
    congregation

FEEDBACK LOOP

1. Staff and Membership Morale
2. Age-Sex Statistics of Membership
3. Percentage of membership drop-
   outs who leave the Church for
   reasons other than moving out
   of the community
4. Number of persons available for
   offices/volunteer service
5. Financial trends
6. Community response
7. Response of other local churches
8. Pastor and staff turnover

results of its programs and services. This information, while readily available, will go unnoticed and/or unused unless the church affects a *feedback loop* to collect, analyze, and interpret the information in such a way as to make it useful for evaluating, planning, and problem-solving.

A Systems Model of a Church

On page 42 is a diagram of a systems model, which shows the interrelatedness of the components that we have described.

A Systems Model of a Typical Local Church   On page 43 is an example of the systems model imposed upon a typical local church. A similar model could be constructed of every subsystem within the church to provide additional information not shown in this model of the local church itself.

You may wish to turn back to page 33 to review the diagram the district superintendent prepared of Community Church. By now we hope you will exclaim: "Aha! That sly fox got the church members in touch with their problems by first leading them into an analysis of their church system and then diagramming their information systematically so they could be helped to sort out the cause of the problem from other circumstances, and to begin working out problem-solving approaches." A review of the Community Church case should now find you able to identify (1) the components of their church system that were the locus of their problems and (2) the problems, as described by the members, that were located in each component.

Throughout this chapter we have stressed the particular emphasis that systems theory places upon the system's mission and environment. We shall now move to a more detailed discussion of these strategic components of the church system.

> Taking a systems approach doesn't create systems.
> It merely allows one to think as things really are.

CHAPTER 4
Mission Intentionality and Systems Theory

Where there is no vision, the people perish.
Proverbs 29:18 KJV

WHY AN INTENTIONAL MISSION IDENTIFICATION?

Many churches would have great difficulty identifying their mission. They are busy trying to solve practical problems but are unaware that behind their problems are questions of mission. Such an approach produces a snowballing effect of more problems, more activities, and an increasing exhaustion for all concerned. George Odiorne suggests: "The typical church is an activity trap. Having lost sight of the higher purposes for which it was originated, it now attempts to make up for this loss by an increased range of activities."[1] Too often, activity is confused with effectiveness. Every local church needs to stop and ask: What are we trying to do? Why? Where are we heading? Even after achieving a set of goals, the church should still ask: So what? Were they worth achieving? Did they move us closer to our mission? A sense of mission focuses on an awareness of direction, purpose, and a reason for being. The mission of the church becomes the standard of measurement for all activity.

On a recent plane trip, I was seated next to a man who was very outgoing and friendly. As I was being seated, he introduced himself and asked me what kind of work I did. When he discovered I was a minister who taught church administration, he responded: "Let me tell you about our church. There is something wrong with us, but I don't understand what it is." He then described their situation, stating that all their board meetings dealt with problems. He identified specific programs that were not working, financial deficits, lack of needed workers, poor attendance, and difficulty in making any decisions. He went on to indicate that he felt their most serious problem was that they had no sense of direction, did not feel they were doing anything important, and their morale was very low. After about an hour's conversation, he concluded they were so over-whelmed with their many little problems that they were unable to focus on the larger wholistic question of why the church really existed and what it was really trying to do. Not being clear on these issues, they had no guidelines for solving individual problems other than to try to relieve the immediate pinch they were feeling at any given time. What he was really saying was that they needed a clear sense of mission. Many local churches suffer from lack of a consciousness of their mission but are not aware of it, like diabetics unaware of their disease in the early stages.

This church was slowed down to near inaction, struggling just to maintain their institution. However, it is possible for a very active, excited congregation also to suffer from mission deficiency. Their condition is not unlike the situation reflected in the story of Wahlstrom's Wonder.

One of the interesting stories coming out of the Korean War is that of a mechanically minded man by the name of Wahlstrom. He enjoyed going to Army surplus sales and buying various intricate electrical and engineering instruments. He would carry them home, take them apart, and put them back together in unique and different combinations. After awhile he had filled an entire room in his home with various sized cogwheels, ringing bells, and lights. As one entered the room, one could push a button, and small, intricate wheels would start to turn. Gradually they would mesh with other wheels until all around the room wheels would be turning and whirring. As the last wheel moved into motion, a light would go on and gradually other lights would intermittently begin to flash on and off throughout the room until the room was lit up like a flashing Christmas tree. As the final lights went on, a bell would begin to ring, and then other bells, until soon the entire room was filled with whirring wheels, flashing lights, and ringing bells.

People were fascinated with this mechanical masterpiece and began to view Wahlstrom as a wonder. One of the townspeople nicknamed the machine Wahlstrom's Wonder. Its fame became widespread, and people began to come from miles around to view Wahlstrom's Wonder.

One day a visitor, impressed by the intricate mechanical responses to the push of a single button, said to Mr. Wahlstrom, "This is really fascinating, but what does it do?" Mr. Wahlstrom explained, "Well, when you push the button the wheels turn, the lights flash, and the bells ring." The man replied, "Yes, I can see that, but what does it do?" And Mr. Wahlstrom replied again, "Well, you push a button, the wheels turn and . . ." In the face of the activity of this mechanical wonder, the question still remained: What function does it perform? What does it do?

There is a parable here about confusing activity with effectiveness in an organization. Could it be that there are churches where the organizational wheels turn, the lights flash on and off in the building, and the bells ring regularly announcing activities and meetings, while people in the community are raising questions about the church: What does it do? Why all the activity? What functions does it perform? Why does it exist?

There are numerous churches that carry on a religious smorgasbord of very active programs and activities with a large number of participants, that could profit by facing the questions: Why? What are we doing? Is what we are doing worth doing? Every church needs to face the question of missional intentionality as to why and how it is in Christian ministry in any specific time and place.

Some readers may be wondering just how it is helpful to a church to develop a conscious intentionality about its mission. One church that found the development of a mission statement a revitalizing and spiritually renewing experience was forced into it by a crisis when suddenly a large percentage of the budget became unavailable because of the moving away of an industry. As the congregation agonized about their future and whether or not they had one, they came to face the question in terms of whether they *should* have a future. This raised other questions like: Why does any church exist? Does God need or call us to Christian ministry in this city, on this corner? What needs exist that this congregation should and can fill? What would be our purpose in going on?

These are the actual, tough questions that the church raised. After struggling with these, the congregation decided to go on, and worked out a statement of their unique mission in that setting. They came to an understanding of why their congregation should continue to exist and what it would accept as its commitment to Christian service and ministry. This mission commitment was followed through and made explicit with concrete goal-setting and long-range planning.

This experience of having to face the issue of the reason for their existence was a turning point in the life of that congregation. Out of it came an awareness of a broader ministry than had been envisioned previously, and the commitment of members to become personally involved in new areas of Christian service and witness. There was a congregational conversion experience. This was evidenced by a membership growth, marked increase in church attendance, and the establishing of new ministries of pastoral concern for persons in a nearby mental hospital and a home for the aging. Within three years this church had, with good response, initiated programs to serve students on the college campus and for meeting community needs. The experience of struggling through and clarifying their mission became the turning point for a renewed and revitalized congregation. In this case, the Holy Spirit was able to use a crisis to bring about a minor miracle. Later in this chapter we will discuss how a congregation can become open to struggling with an awareness of mission without being thrust into it by a threatening crisis.

RELATIONSHIP OF SYSTEM'S THEORY AND MISSIONAL INTENTIONS

A systems view of any organization is concerned with its mission. In chapter 3 we identified the theological-missional purposes of a church as one of the main aspects of its transforming system. Every church must answer the missional question of what it purposes to do, and every organization within the church must be clear as to why it exists and what it expects to accomplish.

A clear missional awareness of what it is seeking to achieve is crucial to the entire transformation process of the church system. The nature of the organizational structures needed to accomplish its task is shaped by what outcomes are desired, what end result the church is wanting to bring about. A clear sense of missional direction is essential for creating effective structures in any systems transformation process.

The same importance of clear missional intention applies to the use of professional and volunteer personnel in the church. The type, skills, quality, and relationships between persons required for the work of the church is essentially determined by what the church is seeking to accomplish and how persons can enable it to achieve its mission.

The key segment of the church's transformation system is its theological-missional purposes. The organizational structure and the utilization of persons are both shaped and harnessed to make this possible.

As a matter of fact, *the dynamic interrelatedness of all components* of the system is the core concept of understanding an organization as a system. It is, therefore, to be expected that the missional purpose of an organization would influence the sorting out of acceptable and unacceptable inputs (*e.g.*, membership requirements, church school materials) in determining the boundaries of the system in relation to acceptable behavioral norms (*e.g.*, gambling, activities for fund raising), and in determining how the parish will relate to specific areas of the environment (*e.g.*, political corruption, community youth program).

The significance of a church's being clear about its missional purposes is being underscored from the perspective of effective systems functioning as well as from a theological and spiritual point of view. From a purely systems perspective, whenever any system is unclear about what it is trying to accomplish (its mission), the impact on the rest of the system will be confusion, fuzziness, frustration, and ineffectiveness.

To clear up any possible misunderstanding, it needs to be stated that a set of specific goals is not a substitute for a mission statement. Goals should be developed from the context of a clear statement of mission. The mission statement gives some parameters for sorting out acceptable goals. It is a standard of measurement for acceptable norms, goals, and activities.

THEOLOGICAL DIMENSIONS OF A CHURCH MISSION STATEMENT

Quite apart from systems theory, each church has another reason for giving attention to clarifying its own mission—a theological reason. Theology is a study of God's activity. God is the source of the Church's existence. The Church, therefore, exists to relate to and to express God's activity in today's world, as well as to interpret God's presence in the past. Hence it is impossible for a church to attempt to function effectively without having a concept of mission. Its concept of mission may be very hazy or very sharp, conscious or unconscious, but every local church has some assumptions that guide its actions. We are saying that every church requires a clear, intentional mission commitment that is undergirded theologically and is open to the Holy Spirit. Any serious attempt to develop such a mission statement will need to take the following sources seriously: *programs*

1. *Bible Study.* The scriptures contain a wealth of material portraying many images and concepts of the Church as God working through his people. A series of sermons on the nature of the Church, with discussion feedback, is one approach to exploring them. Another is for members of a group to share biblical material that the Spirit has made meaningful to them. A Bible study group under trained leadership is also helpful. Resources for biblical study are listed in the footnotes.[2]

2. *Theological and Doctrinal Concepts of Church.* Serious explorations of the mission of the Church must include exposure to doctrinal and theological studies of the Church's nature and purpose. Historical and contemporary scholars alike are fruitful resources.[3] Both historic and contemporary expressions of the meaning of the Christian faith are stimulating for one's own personal reflection.

3. *Tradition.* Each denomination has a statement setting forth its concept of the Church, summarizing the tradition of that branch of Christianity. Each local church should become familiar with its own tradition and that of others as well. The field of Church history offers a wealth of material on how the Church has struggled to define its nature and mission throughout the centuries.

4. *The Needs of the World and Contemporary Society.* "God loved the world so much that he gave his only Son" (NEB). Since God's ministry is to the world, and since we are his ambassadors, the ministry of the local church must also be to the world. The Bible and the history of the Church are records of God at work at a given point in time. The Church's existence is an ongoing witness to God's presence in the world. Hence any contemporary statement of the Church's mission must take into account the present world situation and the culture of our own time.

Today's needs do affect the *form* of Christian witness called for by today's Church.

5. *The Local Scene.* Even more specifically, a local church must identify those areas of local community and personal life to which the congregation must address itself in its ministry. The New Testament is quite clear that Jesus addressed his ministry to particular persons in specific situations. The local church must ask, To whom is our ministry and mission to be addressed?

6. *The Presence of the Holy Spirit.* God's living presence is at work today expressing itself in contemporary life. The parish must keep open to the presence of the Holy Spirit as it seeks to clarify its mission. This requires a continuous sensitivity to God's Spirit and an openness to change as situations and God's Spirit directs.

The development of a local church mission statement is essentially an answer to the question, What is the meaning of being in Christian ministry right here and right now? *Maintaining a current mission statement is an ongoing, never-ending theological activity of the local church.*

A MODEL FOR DEVELOPING A CHURCH MISSION STATEMENT

We have developed a process for preparing a congregational mission statement that is proving helpful to a large number of local churches at the time of this writing. These churches are of varying sizes and denominations. Not only are churches able to come up with clear and useful mission statements, but they report that participants are enthusiastic about the process of working out the statement. A diagram of the process is presented on the following page.

The time line for this process will vary with the number of participants. Phase one involves a serious congregational study and discussion of the nature and mission of the church that might include sermon talk-backs, small discussion groups, or a retreat. Phase two involves an overnight retreat to develop a mission statement. This design requires a

A PLANNING MODEL TO DEVELOP A MISSION STATEMENT

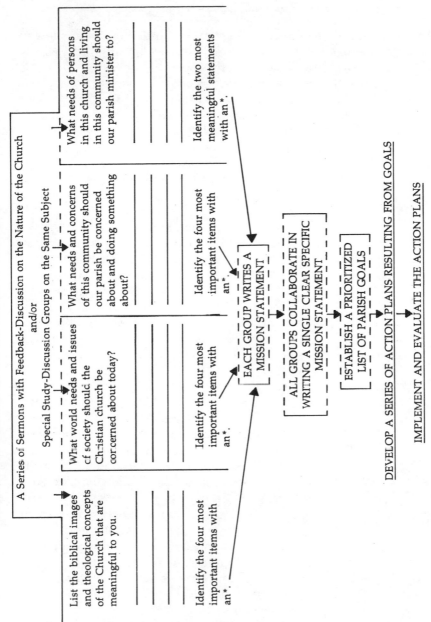

A Series of Sermons with Feedback-Discussion on the Nature of the Church
and/or
Special Study-Discussion Groups on the Same Subject

List the biblical images and theological concepts of the Church that are meaningful to you.

Identify the four most important items with an*.

What world needs and issues of society should the Christian church be concerned about today?

Identify the four most important items with an*.

What needs and concerns of this community should our parish be concerned about and doing something about?

Identify the four most important items with an*.

What needs of persons in this church and living in this community should our parish minister to?

Identify the two most meaningful statements with an*.

EACH GROUP WRITES A MISSION STATEMENT

ALL GROUPS COLLABORATE IN WRITING A SINGLE CLEAR SPECIFIC MISSION STATEMENT

ESTABLISH A PRIORITIZED LIST OF PARISH GOALS

DEVELOP A SERIES OF ACTION PLANS RESULTING FROM GOALS

IMPLEMENT AND EVALUATE THE ACTION PLANS

period of several weeks to carry out and should be followed immediately by a goal-setting, action-planning process.

We will briefly describe the model.

Phase I :   Study and Discussion

    1. A series of sermons on the nature and mission of the Church with feedback discussion may open the subject. This will involve the entire congregation.

    2. Special study-discussion groups may be conducted on the nature and mission of the Church, following step one or as an alternate option.

Phase II: Developing a Mission Statement

    1. The administrative board members and all interested members of the congregation are invited to a series of workshop sessions or a retreat to develop a mission statement to be used as a basis for goal-setting and action-planning for future programming.

    2. Divide the total group into small groups of no more than eight. *Each group* will do the following:

Session I

    a. On newsprint, list (brainstorm) the biblical images of the Church and theological concepts group members find most meaningful and relevant.

    b. Take a break, walk around and browse at other lists, return and complete your own list.

    c. Discuss and select the two images or concepts your group finds most meaningful and write them on newsprint.

    d. All groups share their two images and/or concepts and the reasons for their selection.

Session II

    a. Use the same groups, giving each

group three sheets of newsprint with separate headings (questions). They are to brainstorm responses to each question. The questions are:

1) What world needs and issues of society should the Christian church be concerned about today?

2) What needs and concerns of this community should our church be concerned about and doing something about?

3) What needs of persons in this church *and* living in this community should our church minister to?

b. Take a break and scan the lists of other groups.

c. Each group now completes its lists and identifies the top four items on each list with an asterisk.

d. Share those items with other groups.

Session III

Each group places its own newsprint listings for Sessions I and II before them. After reviewing the material, draft a clear, brief statement of no more than a few sentences beginning, "The mission of our church is ——————————————." Share the statements of each group with the total group by having them read, and then post them in the room.

Session IV

Each group elects two persons (one person if there are more than six groups) to "fishbowl" in a collaboration session to work out a single mission statement for all groups. The mission statements of *each* of the groups must be posted in plain view. Blank newsprint will be posted to work out

the single statement. The fishbowl group
will sit in a circle in the center of the room
with two empty chairs. Members of the
original groups will sit next to one another in
a larger circle surrounding the fishbowl
group. Any person may move into one of the
two empty chairs to ask a question or make a
suggestion; he then must move out. Every
fifteen minutes the collaborators from each
group will go back to their original group for
suggestions. The process goes on until a
mission statement is agreed upon by the
collaborators, checking it out with each
group.

Members of the congregation should be
especially urged to attend this session, to
form groups of eight, and to participate in
the fishbowl collaboration session. This is
likely to be a long session requiring two or
more hours of time, as will likely be true of
each of the three other sessions.

The time structure of each session may be
altered to fit the needs of the situation. The
larger the number of participants, the more
time the design will take. The design can be
carried out at an overnight retreat or in three
separate sessions.

It is also possible for organizations within
the church to adapt this design to their own
planning needs.

PRACTICAL USES FOR AN INTENTIONAL MISSION STATEMENT

There are those who question the value of
developing a mission statement. Some feel that certain
denominations moved in this direction a few years back with
little effect. No doubt the same might be said about the

church's witness for peace or social justice. Nevertheless, they remain valid concerns today. Previous denominational emphasis on mission statements tended to flow from the top down to the local church, and this engendered no small degree of resentment. Much of the content material for the mission statement was also handed down. It was as though the local church was putting together a pre-fab "mission kit" with the conclusions preshaped by the hierarchy. We are proposing a search for mission on the part of each local church using only broad guidelines, with all the decision-making done in the local church. We are suggesting not a denominational but a local move toward a mission statement. Systems theory suggests that each local church has unique qualities and a unique mission.

Others have questioned whether it can be demonstrated that a specific biblical image or theological concept of the Church implicitly requires a particular structure or program or, at the other extreme, whether almost any program would be appropriate for a given concept, *e.g.*, "body of Christ" or "people of God."

In our view, it is neither wise nor necessary to try to make a case that a particular passage either requires or negates any specific church structure or organization. The value of biblical images is not in the structures they suggest but in the meaning they carry for persons about the Church's identity as to who or what the Church should be and what the Church should be doing. Our stance would be that a mission statement need not be based upon or limited to one biblical passage. Paul Minear has identified more than two hundred biblical images of Church.[4] The wealth of available biblical material is such that, in different times and places, different images become appropriate, with changing circumstances calling for special attention. In addition, other factors also enter into developing a mission statement including tradition, doctrine, contemporary world needs, the local situation, and the presence of the Holy Spirit.

Probably the most important reason that efforts to develop mission statements in the past were not as helpful as they might have been is that they were not viewed or utilized as part of a dynamic systems approach to the Church as an organization. Unless the mission statement evolves out of grass-roots planning it will be of little value.

We shall conclude this chapter by indicating how an intentional mission identification by a local church relates to other components of its system.

When a local church has clearly indicated what it considers its mission to be—what it exists to do—the impact of that decision will be evident throughout the system. First of all, the church will be better able to pinpoint its desired outcomes through a planning cycle, beginning with a goal-setting process. Such a process will involve the total congregation in sharing individual members' goals for the church. The many suggested goals from the congregation will have to be sorted out, as some will even be contradictory. The mission statement will contribute to setting parameters for acceptable goals and help identify those of prime concern. A mission statement provides the criteria for determining and ordering goals, the stated desired outcomes of a systems view. The clarification of mission equally affects all systems components. We have already mentioned that *organizational structures* are to be set up and/or modified to enable the carrying out of mission, and *persons* are to be related to positions, and to one another, in ways that express mission. Surely many of the *boundaries* of the system are defined by the nature of its mission. Beyond this, the kinds of *inputs* sought to enhance the life of the church, and those rejected as being restraints on achieving mission, are determined by the nature of its mission as identified by the congregation. The most important criterion for deciding how the church should relate to the specific segments of its *environment* is its concept of mission. The church will decide to make a collaborative stance with some other systems in the environment and to take the stance of an adversary in relation to other segments, depending on its understanding of its own mission—what it exists to do.

What has been said in this chapter about the importance of

a local church clearly understanding and identifying its own mission is equally valid for those of a conservative evangelical stance as well as for radical social-action congregations. It is valid for Roman Catholics, United Methodists, Baptists. Every church, large or small, rural or urban, will function more effectively by clearly defining its mission.

Having once defined its mission, a church can and should move on to systematically plan its program, to budget its money, and to use its human resources in such a way that all components and resources of the system are working together to maximize the achievement of its mission. Chapter 6 will present a detailed approach to systemic program planning and budgeting based upon the congregation's statement of mission.

> *Many churches become so engrossed in activity*
> *that they lose sight of their purpose.*
> (Anonymous)

CHAPTER 5

Interaction of Church and Environment

God so loved the world that he gave his only Son.

John 3:16a RSV

One of the most intriguing parables reflecting how environmental realities necessitate changes in behavior is found in Corrigan and Kaufman's "Fable" in *Why Systems Engineering*.[1]

Once upon a time there were two pigs (a third one had gone into marketing and disappeared) who were faced with the problem of protecting themselves from a wolf.

One pig was an old-timer in this wolf-fending business, and he saw the problem right away—just build a house strong enough to resist the huffing and puffing he had experienced before. So the first pig built his wolf-resistant house right away out of genuine, reliable lath and plaster.

The second pig was green at this wolf business, but he was thoughtful. He decided that he would analyze the wolf problem a bit. He sat down and drew up a matrix (which, of course, is pig latin for a big blank sheet of paper) and listed the problem, analyzed the problem into components and possibilities of wolf strategies, listed the design objectives of his wolf-proof house, determined the functions that his fortress should perform, designed and built his house, and waited to see how well it worked. (He had to be an empiricist, for he had never been huffed and puffed at before.)

All this time the old-timer pig was laughing at the planner pig and vehemently declined to enter into this kind of folly. He had built wolf-proof houses before, and he had lived and prospered, hadn't he? He said to the planner pig, "If you know what you are doing, you don't have to go through all of that jazz." And with this, he went fishing, or rooting, or whatever it is that pigs do in their idle hours.

The second pig worked his system anyway, and designed for predicted contingencies.

One day the mean old wolf passed by the two houses (they both looked the same—after all, a house is just a house). He thought that a pig dinner was just what he wanted. He walked up to the first pig's house and uttered a warning to the old-timer, which was roundly rejected, as usual. With this, the wolf, instead of huffing and puffing, pulled out a sledge hammer, knocked the door down, and ate the old-timer for dinner.

Still not satiated, the wolf walked to the planner pig's house and repeated his act. Suddenly, a trap door in front of the house opened and the wolf dropped neatly into a deep, dark pit, never to be heard from again.

Morals: 1. They are not making wolves like they used to.
2. It's hard to teach old pigs new tricks.
3. If you want to keep the wolf away from your door, you'd better plan ahead.

INTRODUCTION

If your church is or has been in a changing community, you have experienced how such an environment affects church life. The wolves huffing and puffing on the church door are indeed not what they used to be, and the changing environment produces new problems requiring new solutions. Some rural areas have seen farms grow larger, population decline, school districts close down, local stores go out of business owing to nearby shopping centers, and youth leave the community permanently after high school.

Many churches in such areas have experienced a serious decline in every area of church life. Some have become members of circuits, sharing their pastors with other churches. Other congregations have merged, and some have closed down. A few have assessed their situation, sought new approaches, and have formed a "larger parish" as one way of seeking to meet the changing circumstances. Usually these larger parishes employ two or more clergy who function as a staff for all the churches. Lay leadership is also shared across the parish, and a parish-wide administrative board makes decisions.

Still other rural areas find themselves engulfed by housing developments, shopping centers, and factories. They become bedroom communities for those who work elsewhere or are escaping the city. In some instances these new residents join the church, bringing with them new ways of doing things that frequently precipitate conflict with the established members. Still other churches find that the incoming new residents ignore their church entirely, saying they feel unwanted or that they don't fit in. In similar circumstances, however, some churches make plans to assist these newcomers to become assimilated into all aspects of community life and the church as well. Specific plans are carried out to involve these new residents in the church's life and in establishing new programs to meet their needs. The new residents become an occasion for renewing and revitalizing the church. It *does* matter how a church responds to changing environment.

There is no doubt about it: rural churches cannot remain the same when the community changes. What happens in each local church depends on the response and reaction of the church to the change in the community.

City churches are likewise experiencing drastic and rapid changes such as: expressways dividing neighborhoods, changing social and economic conditions, shifts in the racial make-up of the community, deteriorating housing facilities, new high-rise condominiums, and zoning changes for industry. In these situations the survival of local churches is threatened. They must reassess the nature of their mission and programs or perish in the wake of environmental change.

One large church standing in a changing downtown city area illustrates this fact. In the midst of a changing environment, it continued to keep up its buildings and to carry on its traditional programs. Its excellent choir continued to sing traditional anthems and to present its annual concert. Faithful adult youth leaders offered games and refreshments regularly, and "important" people of the city continued to serve on the board even though they had moved from the downtown area. These traditional church programs, however, did not attract the new people moving into the neighborhood, nor did they hold the interest of those continuing to live there. The church school finally found itself with only forty students and nearly one hundred classrooms. The membership declined drastically, and financial reserves were exhausted, leaving the church with no alternative but to close. Little effort had been made to relate to the many people moving into the area or the changing needs of the community. The facts are that in a changing environment existing church programs become less and less effective and more and more out of touch with reality.

In contrast to this church is a local congregation in New York City that was founded as a Norwegian-language church for new immigrants. Later, as the first American-born generation grew up speaking English, services were offered in Norwegian and English. After some time, when Spanish-speaking persons moved into the area, the congregation offered their building to them for their services. Currently, persons from India are moving to the area and are now using the facilities. The congregation has seen it as their mission to provide for the needs of new residents in the community. They have been sensitive enough to environmental shifts to retranslate this mission through three neighborhood changes.

Changing environmental circumstances are a reality facing every church—rural, suburban, or city. In addition to changing local communities, worldwide social, political, economic, ecological, and human values are also in flux. The cases cited above indicate that different churches react to the same set of changing circumstances quite differently. If a church is to remain relevant through environmental change, its leaders, lay and clergy, must discover how to deal with the church and its changing environment.

One of the most effective tools available for focusing on the interaction of church and environment is found in systems theory and analysis. This chapter will seek to set forth and apply systems insights to the church-environment interface.[2]

VIEWING THE ENVIRONMENT FROM A SYSTEMS PERSPECTIVE

An organization exists not in a vacuum, but within a context of countless interactive systems. The environment of a church comprises those systems which influence the church and those which are influenced by it or which it is seeking to influence. A pastor can no longer be effective by paying attention to the church only; rather he must:

1. Understand the *nature* of those systems comprised in the environment of the church.
2. Understand the *relationship* of those systems to the church.
3. Be able to create effective church structures and programs that will most likely have the desired impact on those systems.

Changing environmental conditions require changing programs and behavior patterns. In the words of the opening parable of this chapter, "they are not making wolves like they used to."

Too often a church gives attention only to its internal life and structures when planning for the future. It is imperative that it give attention to what is happening in other systems. These other systems are effecting radical changes in society, life-styles, values, and the lives of persons. Such an environment is transmitting signals to the church calling for needed changes both internally and externally. Church leaders must be equipped to pick up the signals and to manage the interaction of church and environment. *This may well be the point of greatest need in church management today.* We believe a systems perspective offers helpful approaches to this problem.

THE CHURCH-ENVIRONMENT INTERFACE

Our environment today is changing *more rapidly* than ever before and in *more unpredictable* ways. Up to now the Church has only had experience in coping with a much slower rate of change where the pace itself gave predictable clues to the direction of change. In today's society, however, rapid, unpredictable change has become a fact of life for nearly all organizations: political, economic, educational, and social, as well as religious. Any planning for the future must, therefore, take into account the *direction, speed,* and *force* with which new changing social and value systems will affect the Church. Though difficult, this assessment cannot be ignored by Church leaders, at least for very long.

Environmental change usually brings feelings of threat and risk to any organization. The Church, like other organizations, requires a degree of internal stability for survival. Therefore, rapid and/or radical change tends to be viewed as disturbing the homeostasis of the Church's life. Frequently conflicts over proposed changes result, bringing their own kind of anxieties and impact on the Church's life.

It is crucial that pastors and lay leaders become skilled in sensing and responding to environmental change early, because later there is a strong tendency to deal with symptoms rather than underlying causes of change. Environmental factors are frequently the underlying causes for changed behavior in the internal life of the church. For example, the cause for the scarcity of young adults in a church's programs may be related to changing environmental factors such as population trends, life-styles, values, mobility, or the economy, as well as to the existing young adult program. The point is, church leaders must develop skills in becoming sensitive to relevant environmental factors and in interacting with them.

Environmental forces must be viewed from two basic perspectives:

1. Worldwide environmental changes affecting all systems and persons everywhere.
2. Specific environmental factors in a local community influencing the local church.

Church leaders need to be in touch with the overarching, worldwide societal changes. Roeber sums these changes up this way.

What are the forces that have brought about these [social changes] . . . ? Social change is the manifestation of shifts in the underlying systems of values, power, and money in society. Many interdependent influences are active: education, rapid communication, transportation, the decline of religion and of the family, increased levels of material aspiration.[3]

He goes on to indicate that "the direction of change is toward more personal freedom." This move toward personal freedom in society is reflected in wider choices of personal life-styles and in increased freedom and liberation for minority groups, women, and others. Organizationally, it is reflected in a strong trend toward a voluntary society, with increased freedom of participation and involvement in decision-making in educational, economic, political, religious, and even military organizations. Each church must reckon with what these changes mean as it interacts with organizations, nations, and persons. More pointedly, it must see what such changes mean for its own structuring and programming. Specific suggestions as to *how* this can be done will be developed in the following section.

BUILDING IN SENSORS TO ENVIRONMENTAL FACTORS

Clergy and lay leaders need to build sensors into the local church organization that will signal the significant environmental changes to which it needs to be alert. This is important because "different external conditions might require different organizational characteristics and behavior patterns within the effective organizations."[4] Appropriate responses may involve either adapting to and utilizing environmental change, or mobilizing resources to counteract the change. In any case, sensitivity to the environment is required for effective functioning.

We suggest four components of a sensoring system to help keep a church (or its subsystems) alert to environmental factors affecting its functioning. These components will assist in gathering accurate and timely information about environmental change.

1. *Structure Ongoing Feedback into the System.* Every organization within a church needs continuous and accurate feedback. Honest, open, critical feedback is not likely to be forthcoming unless it is structured into the operational process. Feedback needs to include *all* the following factors:

   a. Internal self-evaluation of mission, structure, programs, and leadership by all participants.

   b. External evaluation from denominational supervisors, colleagues, and outsiders.

   c. Periodic organized data-gathering from members, with particular attention to nonactive members.

   d. Leaders being sensitive in personal conversations with anyone willing to offer open, honest, critical feedback.

Whenever feedback is received, it needs to be taken seriously, evaluated, and acted upon.

Sometimes the clearest feedback is *behavioral* in nature and may come from inside or outside the church. *Behavioral signals* include: complaints, absences, reduced participation, financial withholding, declining volunteer leadership, irritating behavior, withdrawal of membership, poor attendance, inability to attract new members, persons' turning elsewhere to have needs met, population segments' (racial, poor, youth, etc.) rejecting the church, etc. Such feedback clearly signals a need to diagnose what is going on within the organization, and how it is relating to its various environmental systems. In summary, one means of sensing environmental changes is to build an effective feedback loop into the system.

2. *Utilize a Participative Decision-Making Process.* Another way to gain current and accurate information about environmental changes is to utilize broad participation in the decision-making processes of the church and its subsystems. Dr. Robert Duncan suggests "greater participation in decision making may increase the information processing potential . . . as well as providing more sources of feedback."[5] Any church is likely to have a broad spectrum of every segment of society in its membership or at least in its constituency. If representatives of these groups (*e.g.*, youth, ethnic, female, male, various vocational, age, educational level) are made members of decision-making groups, they will serve as linking persons[6] with many environmental systems. This process should be consciously utilized to enhance the church's sensitivity to and interaction with its environmental systems. This could assist the church both in meeting the needs of its own members and in designing outreach thrusts to affect various segments of its environment.

3. *Intentionally Develop Contacts and Resources in Relation to Other Relevant Systems in the Environment.* Church leaders and members should be in communication with other systems in its environment: cultural, economic, technical, educational, and political. Being in communication with these systems will add much important information to the church and may open many doors to available resources. Specific persons in these systems need to be sought out for input regarding the church's mission and programs.

4. *Develop a Systems-Environment Matrix for the Church and Its Major Subsystems.* The environment in general is too broad for a church to relate to. Each church, therefore, must identify precisely the systems and subsystems in its environment that are affecting its own functioning. Likewise, it must identify those systems it wishes to affect and change. After identifying the specific environmental systems and subsystems that affect the functioning of the local church, relevant information for planning can be gathered and processed for affecting future changes in the church.

A MODEL OF THE PARISH-ENVIRONMENT INTERFACE

A diagrammatic systems model has been developed to help pinpoint the sociocultural, economic, personal, and organizational segments of the environment that most directly affect church life. The matrix form (page 70) lists the specific systems in the environment that one local church board identified as being comprised in the immediate environment of their church. You are encouraged to construct such a matrix of your church and its environment.

It is important for those using such an instrument to be as specific as possible in identifying the relevant segments of the environment. After the matrix is completed, full discussion of the perceived implications of each item will contribute much to helping the church or one of its subsystems relate to these segments of its environment.

THE IMPACT OF ENVIRONMENTAL CHANGE ON THE CHURCH

Environmental change is the prime initiator of change within most organizations. The Church is no exception. Many scholars agree we are living in a time of the most rapid,

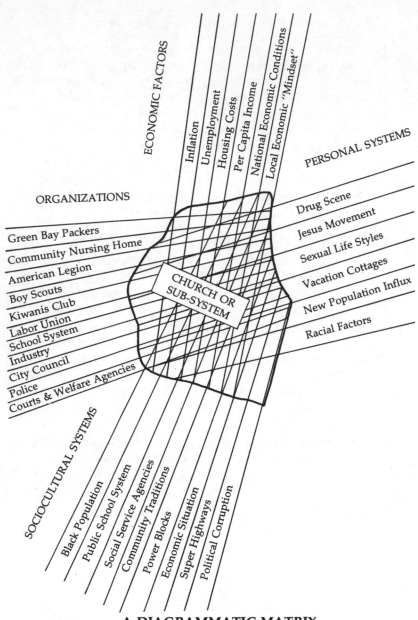

ECONOMIC FACTORS

Inflation
Unemployment
Housing Costs
Per Capita Income
National Economic Conditions
Local Economic "Mindset"

PERSONAL SYSTEMS

ORGANIZATIONS

Drug Scene
Jesus Movement
Sexual Life Styles
Vacation Cottages
New Population Influx
Racial Factors

Green Bay Packers
Community Nursing Home
American Legion
Boy Scouts
Kiwanis Club
Labor Union
School System
Industry
City Council
Police
Courts & Welfare Agencies

CHURCH OR
SUB-SYSTEM

SOCIOCULTURAL SYSTEMS

Black Population
Public School System
Social Service Agencies
Community Traditions
Power Blocks
Economic Situation
Super Highways
Political Corruption

A DIAGRAMMATIC MATRIX
OF CHURCH-ENVIRONMENT INTERFACE

radical, and pervasive change in history, and all indications are that this change will accelerate in the next fifty years. Alvin Toffler's well-known book *Future Shock* illustrates how rapid and anxiety-producing such changes in our society may be.

These environmental changes confront the Church with inescapable decisions. Society continuously faces new problems and circumstances. If the Church does not refocus its programs and services to meet the emerging needs of persons and society, it will soon find itself out of touch with life. No contemporary organization can ignore the pervasive recent changes identified below.

ENVIRONMENTAL CHANGES IN KEY SYSTEMS IN RECENT YEARS			
Technical	Social	Organizational	Personal
—Atomic and nuclear power —Space exploration —Computer science —Air transportation —Electronic advances —Television and communication —Medical discoveries	—Advancement of human rights —Liberation movements —Minority group power —Meaning of war —Environmental threat —Equal housing and education —Government concern for social welfare and human rights —Energy crisis —World hunger	—Rise and independence of small nations —Political shift of power —World economic structures —Educational revolution —Participative decision-making in government, industry, and education	—New life-styles —Increasing affluence —Sexual revolution —Women's liberation —Black and minority liberation —Family changes —Values changes —Individual freedom

This list is only a beginning, but there is hardly an organization or system that has not been brought to the threshold of radical decisions because of these environmental changes. Think of how some of these have affected the Church. In these times when the needs of society and

71

persons are in continuing flux, the Church must change its programs and outputs in order to remain relevant and effective. As a policeman said to a group standing on a street corner during a riot, "If you're gonna stand around here, you've got to keep movin'." So it is with the Church today.

To accomplish its mission, the Church must not simply respond to change, it must also initiate action to affect and influence other systems and to serve persons outside its membership. An important part of its mission is to move in on the prevailing atmosphere of rapid change with its own impact.

The view a local church holds regarding its environment in relation to its assessment of its own strength greatly affects every other part of its life. Four basic viewpoints or various combinations of them may be held:
1. A high regard for its systems' resources (strengths).
2. A high regard for the environment.
3. A low regard for the environment.
4. A low regard for its systems' resources (*i.e.*, a sense of weakness).

Any particular combination of the above perspectives affects the dynamics of a church's reaction to its environment. As a matter of fact, this combination affects the leadership style, the organizational climate, and the goals and programming of the church.

The diagram on page 73, suggested by Dr. Douglas Lewis, depicts the expected interaction of a church with its environment, based upon the view it holds of itself and of its environment.

To interpret the diagram, read the response identified in any quadrant as reflecting the dynamic engendered by the high or low regard for environment and for its own resources identified at the four outside corners. For example: a church with a high regard for its systems' resources *and* a high regard for the environment will be expected to manifest an interactive stance in relation to the environment.

What is being suggested is that the pastor's (or group's) attitude toward the church and the environment is reflected

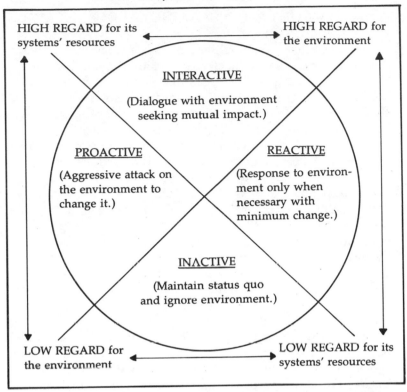

HIGH REGARD for its
systems' resources ⟷ HIGH REGARD for
the environment

INTERACTIVE

(Dialogue with environment
seeking mutual impact.)

PROACTIVE

(Aggressive attack on
the environment to
change it.)

REACTIVE

(Response to environ-
ment only when
necessary with
minimum change.)

INACTIVE

(Maintain status quo
and ignore environment.)

LOW REGARD for
the environment ⟷ LOW REGARD for its
systems' resources

SYSTEMS ⟷ ENVIRONMENT INTERFACE

in the behavior described in each of the quadrants. This
dynamic is also evident in the organizational climate. The
leadership approach the pastor or lay leader takes reflects the
quadrant one perceives himself or herself to be in. To change
a church's interaction from pro-active, interactive, reactive,
or inactive, a change in attitude or point of view must take
place relative to the regard the church has for its environment
or its organizational resources. This is an important clue for
church leaders. A basic factor affecting the changing of a
church's relationship to the environment is the attitude the
leader and members hold about the church and its environment.

A FUTURES PLANNING GROUP IN THE CHURCH

Each local church must choose to be pro-active, interactive, reactive, or inactive in a changing environment. If it waits to see what is happening in the environment by being inactive or reactive, two hazards are involved. One is that its program will be determined by the environment. The other is that the church will always be one step behind its rapidly changing environment. In contrast, the church can opt to be interactive or proactive and use its energy, resources, and personnel to shape the future. Even though this is difficult, it is possible.

It has been rightly said, "The future is hidden in our midst, but we have difficulty seeing it because we respond to the new always in terms of our *past* experience."[7] Operating in the context of past experience tends to link us to tradition, limit our vision, build in a resistance to change, stifle creativity, and cause resistance to new ways of thinking. Too frequently, stability has meant maintaining the *status quo*. *Stability needs to be retranslated to mean reshaping the church to function in changing times so that it will continue to be a viable institution in the future.*

If the future really is hidden in our midst, how can it be uncovered? One approach that has proved helpful has been to create a futures planning group for the local church. Participants in the process should include the most knowledgeable persons in the church, and nonmembers with special knowledge in key areas of the environment. These key environmental areas for the local church should have been identified by previously developing the church-environment interface diagram illustrated on page 70.

Allow time for the future's planning group to function as a think-tank team in projecting probable future changes in key environmental areas most likely to affect the church. Following this, the group develops alternative approaches the church may initiate in relation to the predicted future directions of its environment. In pursuing its task, members of the group will need to help one another move beyond traditional modes and thought patterns in order to develop innovative and nontraditional responses. If this process is done within the clear context of mission, it will give the church a basis for specific action planning geared toward shaping the future.

A MATRIX FOR INITIATING FUTURE CHANGE AND GROWTH IN THE CHURCH

The process described on following pages has been helpful to church groups in planning the future expansion of programs and services. This model can enable a group to move beyond traditional thought patterns and into new ways of conceptualizing programs. It has proved especially useful in stimulating responses in brainstorming sessions focusing on future programs to meet emerging needs. The model rests on the premise that change and growth result from securing the participation of present members *and* of new persons in new programs and services of the church.

A church experiencing an environmental crunch and desiring to expand its outreach and ministry has these options:

1. To seek new participants for its present programs and services from within its active membership.
2. To seek new participants in its present programs and services from its inactive members.
3. To modify or improve its present programs and services to make them more appealing to:
   a. present active members.
   b. present inactive members.
   c. nonmembers in the community.
4. To introduce a totally new program or service designed to appeal to and meet the needs of any of the above three groups.

Obviously, initiating a totally new service or program designed to appeal to totally new persons (nonmembers) carries the greatest risk because of all the unknown factors involved. Yet such planning may have the greatest potential for survival and growth, especially if the present programs and services are not appealing to nonmembers in the community, and if the new programs and services succeed in meeting the felt needs of this group.

Based on the material above, we have developed a matrix that has proved helpful in stimulating brainstorming responses in the future's planning groups in both rural and urban churches seeking new missional ways to respond to a changing environment. The matrix is designed to be used following the group's development of the Church-Environment Interface instrument on page 70. The two instruments together have proved to be excellent systems tools for dealing with the interaction of church and environment.

The following brief instructions will prepare you for using the instrument. The process is to move from the familiar to the unfamiliar.

1. *Brainstorming*
   a. Brainstorm programs and services for every situation indicated on the matrix. Begin with top left-hand square for present active members and move across the top row.
   b. Next, move to the middle row and brainstorm your way across the three columns.
   c. Finally, move across the lower row, thinking creatively and in totally new dimensions on how to reach and serve new persons and situations in the light of the changing environment surrounding your church. Note that the further down and to the right you move, the more unfamiliar the ideas become and the greater the risk.
2. *Evaluating*
   Evaluation of any brainstorming suggestions should be withheld until the matrix is completed. After the brainstorming is completed, the group should evaluate the responses *in the same order as listed.*

MATRIX FOR CHANGE AND GROWTH IN THE PARISH

EXPANDING PROGRAMS AND SERVICES FOR MISSION →

	PRESENT PROGRAMS	MODIFY SERVICES & PROGRAMS	INTRODUCE TOTALLY NEW PROGRAMS AND SERVICES
OBJECTIVES TO PRESENT ACTIVE MEMBERS	Sunday Morning Worship.	Hold a Sermon Talk Back after Sunday Worship.	Initiate Short Term Week Night Bible Study Group.
TO INCREASE PARTICIPATION OF INACTIVE PRESENT MEMBERS	Hold Neighborhood Meetings to get Acquainted.	Survey Inactive Members for Change Suggestions to Meet Their Needs.	Start a church Bowling League.
TO REACH AND SERVE NEW PERSONS AND SITUATIONS	Do Sustained Lay Calling Throughout the Neighborhood.	Offer Use of Building for Community Youth Center.	Identify Specific New Groups of Persons to be Served and Get Their Suggestions.

INCREASING RISK →

3. *Action Planning*

 The entire input of the futures planning group should be referred to the administrative board for discussion, planning, and *action*.

The matrix contains only one illustrative idea in each square. Your group, of course, should brainstorm as many suggestions for programs and services in each square as possible.

In our experience, when a futures planning team, composed of key church members *and* persons from the significant environment segments, form a think-tank group to use this instrument, something significant happens. The process will provide the church with useful suggestions and information for relating to and affecting its environment. However, unless the results are given to the church administrative board for translating into action plans, nothing will happen.

> *Be wise as serpents and innocent as doves.*
> Matthew 10:16 RSV

CHAPTER 6

The Program-Planning and Budgeting System

*Man plans his journey by his own wit, but it is
the Lord who guides his steps.*

Proverbs 16:9 NEB

INTRODUCTION

The same question can be asked of systems theory
that was asked of Wahlstrom's Wonder: This is really
fascinating, but what does it do? Or, to put it another way:
Systems theory has developed some tantilizing concepts, but
really now, what can it do for me? Well, for one thing,
systems theory has produced a number of management tools
that may help you be more effective in your efforts to
motivate and mobilize your church for significant
ministries—tools that may help you find some answers to
your most perplexing leadership questions, such as: How
can I motivate more of our members to serve on church
committees? How can I get the church to plan its budget
based upon what it wants to accomplish in the future, rather
than how much it cost to keep the doors open last year? How
can we get interest and vitality in our administrative board
meetings? How can we solve this problem?

TWO IMPORTANT MANAGEMENT FUNC-TIONS: GOAL SETTING AND PROBLEM SOL-VING

The most important act of organizational leadership a pastor can perform is assisting the church to set missional goals and motivating the people to accept the goals and work toward them. The second most important management act, and closely related to the first, is assisting the church in analyzing and solving its organizational problems. Formulating goals and problem analysis are management functions that should be carried out rationally and systematically.[1] Yet, lacking any tools to assist in this effort, many pastors attempt to "fly it by the seat of their pants," hoping, and sometimes even praying, that this time they might be lucky. More is needed in goal-setting and problem-solving than luck, however, or even experience. If one wants to, almost any pastor can recall from his or her own experience a long list of bungled problems and wrong decisions. The more years of experience, the longer the list.

There is certainly more involved in being an effective pastor-manager than the ability to think through problems and to set goals systematically. Nonetheless, the ability to do systems planning and problem-solving is unquestionably a basic necessity for any pastor who hopes to manage well.

Systems theory provides many tools for planning and problem-solving in the church. We will present two of these tools: Program Planning and Budgeting System (PPBS), a planning process; and Problem Analysis, a problem-solving process (in the next chapter).

PROGRAM PLANNING AND BUDGETING SYSTEM: A PLANNING PROCESS

Zion Church Discovers a Better Way

Except for one incident, the annual business meeting at Zion Church had been like all business meetings for as far back as anyone could remember. Pastor Dave had opened the meeting by saying something about it being regrettable that so few members were there to deal with "these important business issues," but since there was a quorum present they would proceed. This was followed by a series of reports about what had been done by various departments and committees over the past year. Mrs. Jackson, the Sunday school superintendent, had stated in her report that the enrollment had dropped from a total of eighty-six a year ago to a present total of seventy-one. She also reported it had cost four hundred dollars to operate the Sunday school, and, owing to the rise in material costs, the Sunday school committee had been forced to discontinue ordering the scripture leaflets and the senior-high paper. She stated, however, that this was probably not too serious since most of the senior high students did not read the paper anyway.

Following the reports, the nominating committee read their slate of nominees for the next year. Since there were no nominations from the floor, the entire slate was elected in a few minutes. It did take a little longer, however, to convince Mr. Jones to continue being the church treasurer. Immediately following the election, he asked to be replaced and was persuaded to keep the job only after several persons had asked him to serve for at least one more year.

The last item of business was the adoption of the budget. Bill Weber, finance committee chairperson, began his report by saying: "Well, as you can see the budget is bigger than last year. We really tried to hold the line. Basically we took the same figures as last year except for utilities, which we increased by five hundred dollars because of rising costs. We also figured a 5 percent increase in the pastor's salary. The biggest dollar increase, of course, is in our denominational askings. Every year they keep asking for more, and I suppose if we are going to be a part of the denomination we have to pay our taxes." A motion was made to adopt the budget as presented, and it looked like the meeting would end on about the same downbeat as it had begun. But as it happened, Shirley Abbot stood and said, "I am not in favor of this budget, and I ask every member here *not* to approve it!"

After a second or two, Shirley continued: "I know Jesus said something about not letting the right hand know what the left hand was doing, but I really don't think he was telling us how we ought to conduct our church business. That's the way we do it though—one group never knows what the other groups are doing! I'm on the pastor-parish committee, and we recommended a 10 percent increase in the pastor's salary. The finance committee, however, budgeted only a 5 percent increase because, as Bill said, they are 'trying to hold the line'! I never knew until now that they were planning a different figure than what we had requested. Shouldn't we talk about these things? Shouldn't the pastor-parish committee know what the finance committee is doing?

"Tonight," she continued, "Mrs. Jackson reported our Sunday school has slipped from eighty-six to seventy-one members. She also said they have had to eliminate some Sunday school materials because they don't have enough money. The finance committee, however, budgeted the same four-hundred-dollar figure for the Sunday school. I wonder, did the finance committee talk to the Sunday school officers before they prepared the budget? And if the cost of materials continues to rise, what will the Sunday school eliminate next year? But what I really wonder is, How concerned are we about the loss of Sunday school members? I'm sure we're all concerned, but we haven't talked about it. Maybe we should. Maybe before we approve the budget we should all talk about it, and instead of trying to hold the line to a four hundred-dollar-budget we should come up with plans to increase our Sunday school enrollment and then budget enough money to make the plan happen. I think we have simply got to stop having one group prepare the budget without talking first to the other committees. Somehow our plans, our needs, and our budget have got to come together more than they do. Our right hand needs to know what our left hand is doing."

The budget was approved, but only after it was decided to increase the Sunday school budget to five hundred dollars, and Pastor Dave had agreed to present some suggestions at the next board meeting about how the finance committee might better communicate with the program committees in preparing next year's budget.

Now it was the morning following the meeting, and Dave was in his office reflecting on Shirley's comments. He agreed with her, of course. He had always felt that the church should set goals and that the budget should somehow be based upon those goals rather than the one question that seemed always to determine it: Well, how much did it cost us last year to pay the bills and keep the doors open? He was determined to make a good report to the board. Perhaps this was an opportunity for change. He would do his homework. He would be ready.

Two months later, Dave was feeling good when he walked into the board meeting. He was ready. "Friends," he said as he began his report, "I have discovered a process that is intended to help a church do more effective planning and budgeting. It is called a program-planning and budgeting system." Then stepping to the blackboard, he wrote,

A *system* is a set of
    coordinated components that
        work together to accomplish a
            common objective.[2]

"I have been doing some study of organizational systems and have prepared a poster diagram of the components of an organizational system." (See page 84.)

After posting the diagram, Dave gave a brief description of each component and its interrelatedness with the others.[3]

Having completed his introduction to systems theory, and answering a few questions, Dave said: "The importance of

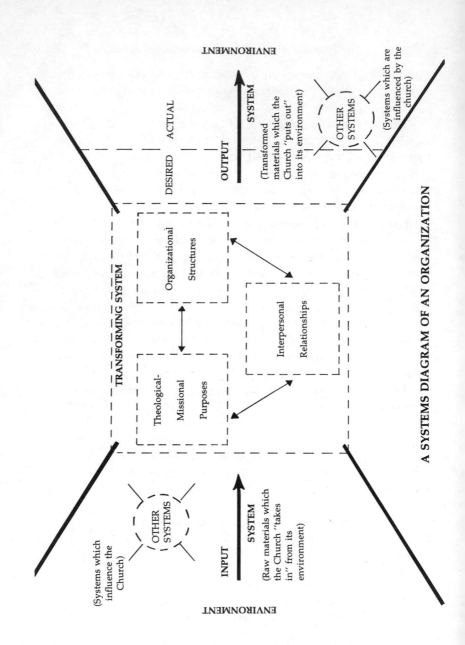

ENVIRONMENT

OUTPUT   **SYSTEM**

DESIRED   ACTUAL

(Transformed materials which the Church "puts out" into its environment)

OTHER SYSTEMS

(Systems which are influenced by the church)

TRANSFORMING SYSTEM

Organizational Structures

Theological-Missional Purposes

Interpersonal Relationships

OTHER SYSTEMS

(Systems which influence the Church)

INPUT   **SYSTEM**

(Raw materials which the Church "takes in" from its environment)

ENVIRONMENT

A SYSTEMS DIAGRAM OF AN ORGANIZATION

this kind of thinking for us tonight is perhaps already becoming apparent. We can, and perhaps should, take a systems approach in conducting our church business. For example, if we were to use this same diagram to help us find a way to do more satisfactory church planning and budgeting, what do you think each of these components would be composed of?"

He then asked them to work for twenty minutes in groups of three to prepare a description of each of the components as they might pertain to a PPBS for their church. After having the time to discuss the material in small groups, the group was able, with a good deal of help from Dave, to define a PPBS as follows:

Environment of a PPBS   The environment comprises those systems in a church which would be influenced by the PPBS or which would have influence upon it, and therefore would need to be involved in the planning process, such as the administrative board, council on ministries, Christian education department, Sunday school, finance committee, worship committee, building and grounds committee, missions committee, pastor-parish committee, and so forth.

Purpose of PPBS   The PPBS is intended to provide a structure and process for the church as a whole and for each of its subsystems, to identify its mission or purpose, to plan ways of achieving its purpose, and to tie its budget-building process to its plans. In doing this the PPBS will focus on intergroup communication and decision-making.

Organizational Structures of PPBS

Programs: Centers of activity and/or responsibility in the church that have a specific purpose (mission) can plan to achieve their purposes and establish budgets to achieve their plans; *e.g.,* pastor-parish committee, Sunday school, building and grounds committee, and so on.

Plans: Set of goals and objectives, with action plans to achieve them, that are put together to achieve the mission (purpose) of a program.

Budgets: The allocation of resources to specific goals, objectives, strategies.

PPBS Committee: A group responsible for coordinating the planning and budget-building activity of the program planning groups, facilitating negotiations between planning groups and finance committee, communicating with the congregation, etc.

Interpersonal-Intergroup Relationships: The PPBS is intended to enhance the self-image and effectiveness of each program committee by encouraging it to set clear goals and to prepare its own budgets.

The PPBS is intended to increase communication, trust, and support between program and administrative groups and the congregation by using processes that allow the congregation and the program committees a more significant role in planning and budget building.

Inputs Needed for PPBS

1. A theological-missional statement by the congregation that gives guidance to and establishes priorities for program planning.[4]
2. A set of plans and budgets prepared by each program committee to accomplish the program's specific purpose and to support the congregation's missional priorities.
3. An indication from the congregation regarding the total budget figure it will approve.
4. Guidelines, timetable, training, materials to assist planning groups.

Outputs Hoped For:

1. A clear missional understanding of what the congregation hopes to accomplish within its own system and in its environment.
2. A clear understanding on the part of each program area regarding its own mission and how this relates to the work of all other programs in the church.
3. Clearly established goals and objectives for each program (plans for achieving mission).

4. Carefully planned budgets for each goal, each program, and finally for the entire church program.

5. A communication/reporting process that allows the congregation to approve the budget in the light of specific program plans and objectives.

Dave turned out the lights and began the short walk to the parsonage. It had been an exciting meeting. The board had decided to implement a PPBS in the church and had appointed a PPBS committee with the responsibility of interpreting this action to the program committees and the congregation. It would be a big job, but everyone at the meeting agreed it would be worth it. A new kind of communication and planning had come to Zion.

After several meetings and much study, the PPBS committee prepared a brief descriptive statement of a PPBS, a model, and a flow chart of activities that they used in introducing the new system to the church. Their materials are presented below.

A Description of a Program Planning and Budgeting System

PPBS is a process designed to allow broader participation of the members in deciding the mission and programs of our church, and in allocating resources (money, people, etc.) to them. In seeking to broaden this participation, PPBS concentrates on gathering, organizing, and distributing useful information throughout the entire church system so that individual members and program committees may use it to construct programs and to set goals for the growth of the church and of its individual members.

PPBS will move our entire church toward *decentralization.*[5] Decentralization involves placing the locus of planning and budgeting as close as possible to the congregation itself. The result of this is that:

1. Mission, programs, and budgets are decided by the congregation, or from information taken directly from the congregation.

2. Program plans and budgets are prepared by each respective program committee.

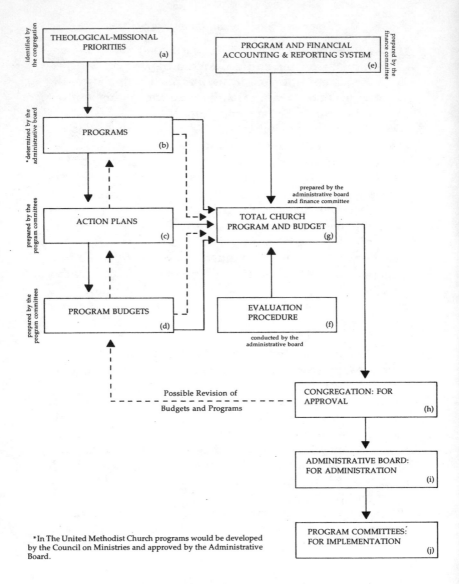

PPBS MODEL FOR A LOCAL CHURCH

Within the figure:

identified by the congregation

THEOLOGICAL-MISSIONAL PRIORITIES (a)

prepared by the finance committee

PROGRAM AND FINANCIAL ACCOUNTING & REPORTING SYSTEM (e)

*determined by the administrative board

PROGRAMS (b)

prepared by the administrative board and finance committee

prepared by the program committees

ACTION PLANS (c)

TOTAL CHURCH PROGRAM AND BUDGET (g)

prepared by the program committees

PROGRAM BUDGETS (d)

EVALUATION PROCEDURE (f)

conducted by the administrative board

Possible Revision of Budgets and Programs

CONGREGATION: FOR APPROVAL (h)

ADMINISTRATIVE BOARD: FOR ADMINISTRATION (i)

*In The United Methodist Church programs would be developed by the Council on Ministries and approved by the Administrative Board.

PROGRAM COMMITTEES: FOR IMPLEMENTATION (j)

3. Administrative committees coordinate the plans and budgets, communicate with the congregation, and seek to provide the necessary resources to ensure success in each of the program areas.

Visualizing a PPBS   PPBS, then, is a process that formulates programs, plans, and budgets at every level of the church system, starting with the congregation, moving through the program and administrative committees, returning to the congregation for final approval, and returning again to the program and administrative committees for implementation. The model on page 88 may prove helpful in visualizing the process used in a PPBS.

The model points to some very important considerations for developing an effective local church program:

1. An effective missional and program strategy cannot be developed in a helter-skelter manner, but requires rational and sequential planning processes.
2. Financial budgets, in order to support the church's mission, need to be prepared for specific plans and programs.
3. Every program committee in the church needs to prepare annual plans (goals and strategies) and budgets.
4. The above considerations indicate that many people and committees need to be involved in formulating the church's programs and budgets. This activity will require coordination and much intergroup communication, which might best be accomplished by appointing a PPBS coordinating committee.

Flow Chart of a PPBS Process

Following is a flow chart of activities that illustrates how the components of the PPBS model are coordinated. We have coded each component on the model by use of a letter—*e.g.*, (a). The same letter will appear on the flow chart to indicate when the flow chart activities coincide with the model components.

A FLOW CHART OF A PPBS FOR A LOCAL CHURCH[6]

WHO	DOES WHAT	WHEN[7]	WHY THIS IS NECESSARY
Congregation	(a) 1. Assesses the needs and opportunities the church has for ministry to its own members and to its environment. 2. Formulates a statement of its theological-missional priorities.[8]	March 1 - April 15	A clear indication of what the congregation sees its needs and opportunities to be, and a statement of the theological-missional priorities it wishes to pursue are the first steps in initiating a PPBS system. This statement will become the measuring stick against which all programs, plans, and budgets will be judged.
Administrative Board	1. Develops categories of the congregation's needs and opportunities for ministry. 2. Formulates broadly stated goal statements within each category which are focused upon the priorities set down by the congregation in its theological-missional statement. 3. Reports its categories and goal statements to the congregation showing how the goals, when reached, should achieve the theological-missional priorities.	April 15 - May 15	Developing the categories and goal statements forces the board to think through the "why" of program activity, to determine whether the activities are coherent with the missional priorities, and to begin the initial work of deciding the church's program for the coming year. The theological-missional statement expresses the congregation's understanding of who it is and why God has called it into existence in this particular time and place. Only the congregation, with the guidance of the Holy Spirit, can decide the crucial question of what programs and activities will best accomplish its mission. Unless the congregation does this important work,

90

| | | May 15—31 | Whatever programs and budgets are finally developed will require the approval and support of the congregation. This activity motivates the congregation's interests and energies toward achieving the goals. People give the strongest support to programs and goals they have helped to formulate. |

| Congregation | 1. Reviews the initial work of the board and makes suggestions for revisions, deletions, or additions of goals. | | |
| | 2. Adopts the revised goal statements as program guidelines for the coming year. | | |

(g)

Administrative Board	1. Reviews the existing program structure[9] of the church to determine: a. Which programs now in existence are needed to continue. b. Which programs are no longer needed. c. What new programs will be needed to accomplish the missional mandate and program targets of the congregation. Appoints new program committees.	June 1—15	To ensure that no ongoing program area of the church becomes trapped in activities without having any specific goals or clear-cut plans, or that any program is not directly supporting the missional priorities of the congregation.
	2. Assigns goal statements to each continuing or new program committee.		
	3. Meets with the program committees to gain their acceptance of the responsibility to achieve the goals.		In order for the program committees to have ownership in goal statements they must fully understand the importance and comprehensiveness of the total program the board is suggesting, and they must have the opportunity to suggest modifications, additions, and so forth.

(Top partial line: "it will never fully understand its purpose and calling.")

WHO	DOES WHAT	WHEN	WHY THIS IS NECESSARY
Finance Committee	1. Polls the congregation to determine a tentative amount of financial support that can be expected, based upon what the congregation now knows about the developing church program.	June 1 - 30	There are usually alternate routes (or plans) a program committee may take to achieve its goals. One important factor in deciding among the alternatives is the amount of money each alternative would require and the total amount the committees and board can reasonably expect they will have to work with.
(Each) Program Committee	(c) 1. Plans its programs for the year by establishing specific goals and objectives and developing step-by-step action plans to accomplish them.[10]	June 15 - August 30	The broad goal statements formulated by the board and approved by the congregation are meant to establish direction for each program, to inform each program committee what the church hopes it will accomplish. It is now the responsibility of the committee to plan how this can best be done and to determine the budget for carrying out their plans.
	(d) 2. Prepares a budget for each goal.		
	3. Submits its program goals and budgets to the administrative board.		
	4. Submits its program budgets to the finance committee.		This process of having several committees planning the church program and budget ensures the greatest amount of wisdom and creativity being put into the planning, and generates the greatest amount of ownership in the plans. The program committees will each be most committed to the plans they have developed.

| | | September 1 - 30 | The various programs must be coordinated into a total package before any judgment can be made about their overall effectiveness, and to be certain the work in each program area will enhance that of the others. |

Administrative Board

1. Coordinates the program plans, removing overlaps, filling gaps, and so on, to finally arrive at a total program that is comprehensive, appealing, and focused on the missional priorities of the congregation.

Finance Committee

September 1 - 20

1. Prepares a tentative total program budget based upon the budgets submitted by the program committees.

Two types of information will be needed for any negotiations necessary for balancing projected costs with projected income:

1. How much income the church can reasonably expect to receive.

2. How much the programs, as planned, plus all other expense items, will cost.

2. Prepares a budget of all administration and buildings and grounds expense items not considered by the program committees.

All expenses in the church are in fact program related; money is spent in support of church programs. The two major expense items of the church are usually seen as "administration" and "building and grounds." These need to be reallocated to the programs in order to provide the congregation and the committees with a much more valid understanding of what each program is actually costing.

3. Reallocates the administration and building and grounds costs to the programs to arrive at a tentative total church program budget.[11]

4. Reports to all committees and the board regarding similarities or differences between the tentative program budget and the projected income, with suggestions for bringing the two into balance.

Following this flow chart is a budget worksheet illustrating the reallocation process. See page 98

WHO	DOES WHAT	WHEN	WHY THIS IS NECESSARY
Administrative Board	1. As is necessary, negotiates with the program committees to revise plans and budgets to affect a near balance between the total tentative budget and the projected income.	October 1 - 31	It is not necessary to arrive at a balanced budget before submitting it to the congregation. If there is too great a difference, however, the congregation will find it difficult to respond.
	2. Submits to the congregation, for review and approval, the total tentative church program and budget, clearly showing each program area, the goals and plans for each program, the budgets for each program.		
Congregation	(g) 1. Responds to the program plans with suggestions, asks questions for further understanding, etc. to determine the extent to which it feels the proposed program is in harmony with its felt needs and opportunities for ministry and its missional priorities.	November 1 - December 15	The congregation is soon to be asked to adopt this program and underwrite its proposed budget. It can only make these decisions in the light of how responsive it sees the program to be to the needs and interests of the congregation and its individual members.
Finance Committee and Administrative Board	1. Gains final congregation approval of the church program, and	November 1 - December 15	Any final budget amount approved by the congregation which is less than the proposed total budget will require the administrative board to negotiate with the program committees for further
	2. Determination and authorization of the final budget.		

Finance Committee and Administrative Board (continued)		revisions of plans to cause the proposed program budget to balance with the total budget amount authorized by the congregation.
Finance Committee	1. Develops and carries out plans needed to secure pledges to assure the financing of the budget and to support the planned programs, or to implement whatever method of securing funds it will utilize.	November 1 - December 15
(Each) Program Committee	(j) 1. Implements their program by focusing on the achievement of their goals and the missional priorities of the congregation.	January 1— Beginning of new program/ fiscal year
Finance Committee	(e) (i) 1. Establishes a procedure for financial accounting according to programs throughout the year.	Can be done any time prior to the beginning of the year.
Administrative Board and Finance Committee	1. Makes regular program and financial reports to the congregation, indicating the progress of each program unit in accomplishing its goals and its budget expenditures.	Having developed the total church budget programmatically, the financial accounting and reporting should be along program lines. This method of reporting will provide the congregation a new and refreshing way of looking at the financial reports and will serve to keep the total church program and its goals freshly in mind.

WHO	DOES WHAT	WHEN	WHY THIS IS NECESSARY
	(f) (i)		
Administrative Board	1. In communication with the program committees, plans a procedure for evaluating the effectiveness of each program area at regular intervals throughout the year.	January 1 - February 28	Evaluation is often a threatening experience, but need not be. A way of reducing its threat and increasing its benefits is to have those whose work will be evaluated to participate in planning conducting, and reporting the evaluation.
Administrative Board	2. Conducts the evaluations and works with the program committees to provide resources, solve problems, readjust plans, and so on to ensure maximum program effectiveness.	Throughout the year	Good evaluation will provide vital information for program control and greatly improve program effectiveness. Evaluation at the end of a program is too late to do much good for that program. PPBS, when once fully established in our church, should operate on a yearly cycle, with the final program evaluation of one year providing valuable planning information for the next.

REALLOCATION ILLUSTRATED

The concept of reallocation is a vital procedure in program budgeting, and one that is very little practiced in local churches. You can gain much help in this procedure by studying a beginning text in cost accounting, available at most college libraries, or by visiting an accountant or accounting professor.

Basically the steps involved in reallocation are:

1. Determining the total costs of the usual administration and building and grounds items.
2. Distributing the total building and grounds cost across the programs and administration, using whatever procedure seems most appropriate—*e.g.*, the percentage of floor space used by each program in carrying out its activities.
3. Distributing the total administration costs across the programs using whatever procedure seems most appropriate—*e.g.*, the approximate percentage of time given to each program by the pastor and staff; the approximate cost of administrative supplies used by each.

On pages 98 and 99 is an illustrated budget worksheet that has proved helpful in reallocating the building and grounds costs and the administration costs to the programs, for showing program budgets, and the line item budget. The worksheet is shown as it might appear for a typical small church.

In addition to illustrating the reallocation procedure, the worksheet illustrates the relationship and differences between a line item budget and a program budget. A careful study of the worksheet would make obvious the ways in which reallocation and program budget reporting provides much more information regarding the church's mission and ministries than does a line item budget alone.

Well, there it is—the process by which the Zion congregation launched their church into a method of planning that was successful in getting many of its committees to set goals based upon the considered interests and theological insights

EXPENSE TYPE	TOTAL	BUILDING & GROUNDS	ADMINIS-TRATION	CHRISTIAN EDUCATION (PROGRAM 1)	WORSHIP (PROGRAM 2)
Pastor's Salary	10,000		1,000	1,000	3,000
Pastor's Benefits	2,000		200	200	600
Clerical Salaries	5,000		1,500	1,000	1,000
Clerical Benefits	500		150	100	100
Maintenance Salaries	8,000	8,000			
Maintenance Benefits	1,600	1,600			
Telephone	600		200	100	
Travel	2,000	300	300		
Office Supplies	1,000		300	200	200
Duplicating/Postage	1,000		200	100	400
Literature	800			600	
Special Events	250			200	
Utilities	4,000	4,000			
Property Insurance	1,000	1,000			
Building Maintenance	2,000	2,000			
Grounds Maintenance	1,000	1,000			
Apportionments	3,000				
SUBTOTAL	43,750	17,900	3,850	3,500	5,300
REALLOCATE BUILDINGS & GROUNDS	- 0 -	-17,900	2,000	7,000	6,000
SUBTOTAL	43,750	- 0 -	5,850	10,500	11,300
REALLOCATE ADMINISTRATION	- 0 -	- 0 -	-5,850	975	975
TOTAL	43,750	- 0 -	- 0 -	11,475	12,275
Line Item Budget		Indirect Costs: Reallocations			

98

OF YOUR CHURCH

MISSIONS (PROGRAM 3)	NURTURE (PROGRAM 4)	YOUTH (PROGRAM 5)	SOCIAL CONCERNS (PROGRAM 6)	(PROGRAM 7)	(PROGRAM 8)
	3,000	1,000	1,000		
	600	200	200		
	1,000	200	300		
	100	20	30		
	200		100		
	1,000	200	200		
	100	100	100		
		100	200		
		100	100		
50					
3,000					
3,050	6,000	1,920	2,230		
- 0 -	1,400	1,500	- 0 -		
3,050	7,400	3,420	2,230		
975	975	975	975		
4,025	8,375	4,395	3,205		

Program Budgets

of the congregation, and to change the entire budgeting process from something that was hurriedly done a day or two before the annual meeting to a significant means for planning the total ministry of the church.

PPBS is a new tool in church circles. It is catching on, however, and across the country congregations are charting new courses for themselves by using the systems approach to planning and budgeting procedures.[12]

CONCLUSION

For the pastor, the primary benefit of PPBS may well be its ability to free him or her from an activity trap that saps one's energy and places ever increasing demands on one's time. Caught in the activity trap, many harried pastors rush madly from one activity to another, too busy to pray, too busy to spend time with their families, too busy to establish personal and professional targets and to take careful aim. PPBS sets the pastor free to participate with the congregation in establishing a clearly defined mission, to establish some realistic goals, and to collect the resources of the entire church around the task of achieving those goals.

If there is any man who fears the Lord,
he shall be shown the path that he should choose.
                              Psalm 25:12 NEB

CHAPTER 7
Problem Analysis

It is pleasant to see plans develop. That is why fools refuse to give them up even when they are wrong.

Proverbs 13:19 TLB

PROBLEM ANALYSIS: A PROBLEM-SOLVING PROCESS

In order effectively to do the work of God in an ever-changing environment, the Church is being called upon to make more decisions more often and more rapidly than ever before. Every change in its environment has its effect upon the Church. Change often causes problems and relegates carefully prepared plans and smoothly running programs to the dung heap of irrelevancy. Problems, problems, problems! Certainly one tool needed by all pastors is an effective means for discovering, defining, and solving problems. Systems problem-solving approaches are by and large the most effective and easily used problem-solving tools available today. In this chapter we shall discuss one such approach.

The components of a problem-solving system are:
1. *Problem Analysis:* identifying and defining the problem and its cause.
2. *Decision Analysis:* planning the course of action most likely to solve the problem.

3. *Implementation:* carrying out the action plan.
4. *Evaluation:* measuring the extent to which the plan is working, and modifying it accordingly.

In this chapter we shall deal with the first component: problem analysis.

THE PROBLEM OF THE MISSING YOUNG PEOPLE

For many years Christ Church had a low number of young people, ages 14 to 21, in attendance at Sunday morning worship. This September only two were attending regularly.

It was now November, and the church leaders were gathered for a weekend planning retreat. After listing several church problems to be dealt with, they decided to tackle the problem of no youth's attending morning worship. Following are excerpts of their conversation:

"Well, the problem is that young people just aren't interested in church and religion nowadays." (Really now, which is the problem: young people's not attending Christ Church in particular, or their not being interested in church in general?)

"I think we've got to get to the parents. If the parents don't make them attend church when they are little, they'll never attend after they get into high school." (Are the parents the cause of young people's not attending?)

"Maybe we need a special service for them. You know, their kind of music and language is different from what we have in church. They like guitars and drums and soul music." (Well now, is the music the problem or the solution?)

"When I was a kid, I hated to go to church. I still remember locking myself in the attic or hiding in the barn until my daddy would get tired of looking and go off to church without me." (How about an evangelistic program? Let's pipe the services into every attic and barn in the whole community!)

"I think we just have to expect it to be this way. A lot of people drop out of church until they get married and have a family. Then they come back." (There it is! The whole thing isn't a problem after all, it's simply nature taking its course.)

COMMON GROUP PROBLEM-SOLVING ERRORS

It sounds as though the group has gone off into the bushes and scared up more rabbits than they can handle, doesn't it? One thing's for certain—what started out as a problem-solving discussion about the absence of young people from the worship services has certainly gone far afield. This discussion, however, is much like many group problem-solving discussions, and perhaps it can serve to provide us some basic insights into the way church committees usually approach problem-solving efforts:

1. They usually deal with problems, causes, and solutions without distinguishing which is which.
2. As they continue the discussion, they jump from one subject to another, and as each new subject is introduced the attention of the group is turned toward it for awhile, only soon to veer away to another newly introduced subject.
3. Members of the group seldom agree on what the "real" problem is because they mean different things when they refer to a problem. Thus, some are discussing problems, some are discussing causes, while others are discussing solutions—all being set forth as the problem.

Since it appears that people tend to confuse problems with causes, and both of these with decisions or solutions, it might be well to set down some basic definitions and concepts for problem-solving before we go any further.

DEFINITIONS

1. Problem: An unwanted effect or an unsatisfied need. As such, a problem is always a *deviation* from a desired performance or result.

2. Cause of a problem: Always an unwanted *change* in some distinctive feature of the system that causes the deviation. This may be a single event or condition, or a combination of events or conditions operating as a single one.
3. Decision: A *choice of action* to solve the problem. A hoped-for solution.

CONCEPTS

We have already mentioned two basic concepts of problem analysis: One is that every problem is a deviation from some desired performance or result, and the other is that a problem is always caused by a change in some distinctive feature or process of the system that causes the deviation.[1] We need, however, to add three more concepts to the list:

1. Every problem has only one real cause, which is either one single event or condition or several that have combined to act as if there were but one single cause. So a search for cause is always a search for one specific change or a combination of changes that have produced the unwanted effect.
2. A problem cannot be solved unless its cause is known. Attempting to solve a problem without knowing its cause is the fundamental reason for failures in problem-solving efforts.[2]
3. A problem is solved by dealing with the event or condition causing it. Emergency, stopgap action may be taken to forestall the consequences of the problem, but the problem will remain until its cause has been discovered and dealt with.

BACK TO CHRIST CHURCH

Now that we are armed with all that conceptual ammunition, let's return to the retreat to see how the problem solvers are faring. You may be heartened to know their group included a person, whom we will call Larry, skilled in problem analysis, who, before the retreat had ended, was able to lead them into some startling discoveries. By asking a series of questions and posting the responses on newsprint, Larry led the group through a logical sequence of steps in problem analysis that enabled them to locate the cause of the problem in one change made ten years earlier.

After the group had wandered afield at some length, jumping from subject to subject, Larry said: "This seems like a complicated and complex problem. It's clear we aren't finding any quick solutions. I think we don't even agree on what the real problem is. We are using a problem-solving approach at work that is proving very helpful in analyzing complex problems. If you would like, I could lead you through the process." The group enthusiastically accepted Larry's offer, deciding they would wait until the next morning to do the analysis.

In preparation for the analysis, Larry posted newsprint across one wall of the meeting room. The next morning he began his work with the group by saying: "There are two fundamental reasons that groups experience difficulty in problem-solving. One, they do not agree on what the problem really is, and two, they tend to jump to conclusions about the cause of the problem before they have got all the information out about it. Problem analysis is simply a disciplined way of getting all the relevant information about a problem before any causes or solutions are considered. We will do the analysis by working our way through a sequence of information-seeking steps. I will write the information you provide on the newsprint so you can visualize the progression of the analysis.[3] Here, on the newsprint, I have prepared a diagram of the steps to be taken in a problem analysis. Perhaps it will be helpful for you to visualize all the steps and their sequence before we begin." (See page 106.)

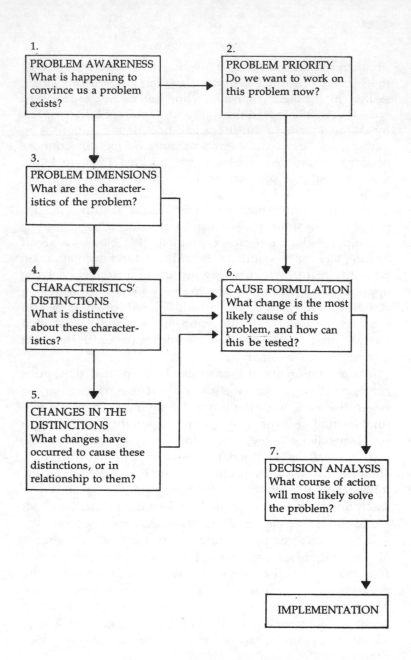

A PROBLEM ANALYSIS MODEL

Following, we shall show the results of the analysis as Larry wrote it on the newsprint. We shall also attempt to explain the problem-solving process by making comments as we go along:

LARRY'S NEWSPRINT (The Six Steps in Problem Analysis)

Our Comments

STEP I: State the problem as clearly as possible.

The first step in problem analysis is to recognize that a problem exists and to state it as clearly as possible.

Christ Church has 22 members ages 14-21. Only two persons in this age group are attending church, however, and neither of them is a member.

A problem is always a deviation from some objective or desired result. The first step in problem analysis is to state as clearly as possible the desired objective and the deviation from it that is to be corrected. This deviation is the problem.

STEP II: Determine the priority of the problem.

The second step in problem analysis is to decide whether you want to work on the problem, postpone it, or ignore it.

A. Any time pressures to solve it?
No deadlines for solving it, but we want to begin now.
B. What will be the effects if it is not solved?
No young people in church now. A declining attendance in the future.
C. Is the situation getting better or worse?

At any one time a church is experiencing more deviations from its objectives than it can possibly give attention to. Deciding to work on one problem almost always carries an implicit decision to postpone or ignore others. Deciding the importance of the problem, therefore, is a must. These three tests—time, effect, and trend—establish

107

Steps in Problem Analysis	*Our Comments*
Gradually getting worse, with sharp worsening this fall.	the importance of the problem in relationship to other problems. Even after a problem has been established as a priority item, it should meet two criteria before any time and resources are committed to solving it. They are: 1. There must be reasonable hope of solving it. If there is no such hope, it should not be worked on, regardless of its priority. To work on such a problem will only dissipate the church's resources and make matters worse. 2. There must be a way of knowing when the problem is solved. Perhaps the only thing worse than attacking a problem and not being able to solve it, is solving it but not knowing it is solved. This, too, will frustrate the church and cause needless expenditure of resources.

PROBLEM ANALYSIS WORKSHEET

Had Larry been prepared to do a problem analysis before he came to the retreat he could have brought with him

PROBLEM ANALYSIS WORKSHEET

PROBLEM:

PRIORITY: Time:
Effect:
Trend:

	What are the DIMENSIONS of the problem?		What is DISTINCTIVE between the two categories?	What CHANGES have occurred to cause this distinction?
A. WHAT/WHO	IS INVOLVED?	IS NOT INVOLVED?		
B. WHERE	DID/DOES IT OCCUR?	DID/DOES IT NOT OCCUR?		
C. WHEN	DID/DOES IT OCCUR?	DID/DOES IT NOT OCCUR?		
D. HOW MUCH/MANY (Extent)	IS INVOLVED?	IS NOT INVOLVED?		
POSSIBLE CAUSES: (* = most likely cause)			HOW CAN MOST LIKELY CAUSE BE TESTED?	

several copies of a problem analysis worksheet for the group's use, which no doubt would have helped them organize their material. On page 109 is an illustration of such a worksheet. As we progress from this point, we shall, between each step of the analysis, indicate how the group's material might have appeared on such a worksheet.[4]

Steps in Problem Analysis	*Our Comments*
STEP III: Determine the dimensions of the problem.	*The the third step in the analysis is to establish the problem's dimensions by specifying precisely what the problem IS and IS NOT, and drawing a boundary that clearly separates the problem from every other activity, issue, or group in the church.*
A. WHAT specific group(s) IS involved? Young people who are members of our church; high schoolers, college students, employed, single, and married, ages 14-21, who do not attend our worship services. WHAT specific group(s) IS NOT involved? 1. The two young people who do attend the services regularly. 2. Other young people, over 21, who attend regularly. 3. Children and youth	Answering the WHAT, WHERE, WHEN, HOW BIG, and HOW MANY questions establishes the problem's dimensions and sets up its boundary showing what information is relevant and what is irrelevant to solving it. The information gathered here, and the boundary separating the deviation from all else, needs to be drawn with such precision that it exposes the change that caused the problem. An inability to identify that change, in Step VI, usually is an indication that the dimensions need to be

Steps in Problem Analysis   *Our Comments*

below 14 who do not attend Sunday school but attend worship with their parents.
B. Specifically WHERE IS the problem located?
In the Sunday morning worship services of Christ Church.
WHERE "IS NOT" this problem in our church?
1. There are 12 young people in this age group attending the Sunday afternoon youth club.
2. Many attend special worship events such as Easter, Christmas.
3. Many attend special events such as weddings.
C. Precisely WHEN DID THIS PROBLEM FIRST OCCUR?
Do not know. Has been a problem for some years.

drawn with more precision and the boundary more tightly.
The answers to these four questions, A, B, C, and D, say everything that can be said about the problem. This is the only relevant information needed to describe it, but remember that information is needed for both what the problem IS and what it IS NOT.
Step III is the single most important step for solving any problem. A problem clearly stated is at least 50 percent solved.

Here is the first question for which the group had no information. After a few minutes, Larry suggested they move on, with the realization that they might very well have to search out the information before any concrete clues about cause could be found.
Interestingly enough, the group soon discovered this question to be vital, and they might have been

PROBLEM ANALYSIS WORKSHEET

PROBLEM: Young people are not attending worship.

PRIORITY: Time: This is one of our most urgent
        Effect: problems, requiring immediate
        Trend: attention.

	What are the DIMENSIONS of the problem?		What is DISTINCTIVE between the two categories?	What CHANGES have occurred to cause this distinction?
A. WHAT/WHO	IS INVOLVED?	IS NOT INVOLVED?		
	Young members, age 14-21, do not attend worship services.	1. Two who do attend. 2. Young people over 21. 3. Youth under 14 do not attend Sunday school.		
B. WHERE	DID/DOES IT OCCUR?	DID/DOES IT NOT OCCUR?		
	In Sunday morning worship services.	1. Sunday afternoon youth club. 2. Special worship events. 3. Other events.		
C. WHEN	DID/DOES IT OCCUR?	DID/DOES IT NOT OCCUR?		
	Don't know when first became serious. Has continued for a long time.	At other worship, social, and youth functions.		
D. HOW MUCH/MANY (Extent)	IS INVOLVED?	IS NOT INVOLVED?		
	22 members, ages 14-21, do not attend regularly.	Two young people do attend regularly.		

POSSIBLE CAUSES: (* = most likely cause)   HOW CAN MOST LIKELY CAUSE BE TESTED?

Steps in Problem Analysis

Our Comments

forced to search for information related to it had not the analysis succeeded in discovering the same information elsewhere.

Precisely WHEN does the problem now occur? At the 10:30 A.M. Sunday worship service.

Precisely WHEN does the problem NOT occur?

At other worship, social, and youth functions.

D. Precisely HOW MANY youth ARE involved in the problem?

Twenty-two members, age 14-21, who do not attend worship regularly.

HOW OFTEN does the problem occur?

Every Sunday morning.

Precisely HOW MANY ARE NOT involved?

Two young persons who attend worship regularly.

These questions are intended to determine the extent of the problem— HOW MANY, HOW MUCH, HOW BIG, and so on.

STEP IV: *Determine the distinctions between the IS and the IS NOT characteristics of the problem.*

This step involves searching out any new or different conditions, or what has changed to produce the distinctions. This is necessary since there is always one certain change,

Steps in Problem Analysis	Our Comments
	or a combination acting as one single condition, that has caused the problem. This change is always in some relationship to a distinction identified in Step IV.
A. What makes the group involved distinctively different from the other groups?	This search for a distinction is a search for dissimilarities and is a style of thinking usually foreign to us. We have been taught to think in terms of similarity and generalizations. Problem analysis searches for distinct dissimilarities and seeks to state them with precision. This step can be greatly facilitated by being very precise and complete in Step III. The sharper the dimensions are drawn between what the problem IS and IS NOT, the fewer the distinctions that will be found. If, after Step III has been done with precision and thoroughness, the distinctions are still difficult to identify, the group has no choice but to dig in and search. A distinction is there and must be found.
1. The non-attenders are members of our church, whereas the two young people who do attend:	
—are not confirmed in our church.	
—are not members of the church.	
—moved into the community this summer.	
2. We do not see any distinctions between the problem group and the young people over 21 years of age.	
3. The children and youth under 14 who attend worship do not attend Sunday school, whereas many of the problem group attended Sun-	

Steps in Problem Analysis	*Our Comments*

day school as children.

These children and youth are not yet confirmed into membership, whereas all of the problem group are confirmed members.

B. What is distinctive about the WHERE of the problem?

See no distinction.

C. What is distinctive about WHEN the problem occurs?

1. It only occurs at Sunday morning worship.
2. This is the only church activity that runs concurrently with the Sunday school hour.

D. WHAT is distinctive about HOW MANY are involved?

This is our total membership between ages 14 and 21.

STEP V: Identify the changes that have occurred to produce the distinctions, or within any area of distinction.

This step, with Step VI, is aimed at finding possible causes by identifying changes in the distinctive areas that possibly could have caused the deviation. This requires

PROBLEM ANALYSIS WORKSHEET

PROBLEM: Young people are not attending worship.

PRIORITY: Time:
Effect:
Trend:
This is one of our most urgent problems, requiring immediate attention.

	What are the DIMENSIONS of the problem?		What is DISTINCTIVE between the two categories?	What CHANGES have occurred to cause this distinction?
A. WHAT/WHO	IS INVOLVED?	IS NOT INVOLVED?		
	Young members, age 14-21, do not attend worship services.	1. Two who do attend. 2. Young people over 21. 3. Youth under 14 do not attend Sunday school.	1. Not confirmed/members, just moved. 2. 3. Non-attenders used to attend S.S.	
B. WHERE	DID/DOES IT OCCUR?	DID/DOES IT NOT OCCUR?		
	In Sunday morning worship services.	1. Sunday afternoon youth club. 2. Special worship events. 3. Other events.		
C. WHEN	DID/DOES IT OCCUR?	DID/DOES IT NOT OCCUR?		
	Don't know when first became serious. Has continued for a long time.	At other worship, social, and youth functions.	Occurs only at 10:30 A.M. Sunday worship, only activity concurrent with Sunday school hour.	
D. HOW MUCH/MANY (Extent)	IS INVOLVED?	IS NOT INVOLVED?		
	22 members, ages 14-21, do not attend regularly.	Two young people do attend regularly.	Total membership, ages 14-21, involved, since two who attend regularly are not members.	
POSSIBLE CAUSES: (* = most likely cause)			HOW CAN MOST LIKELY CAUSE BE TESTED?	

Steps in Problem Analysis	*Our Comments*
	carefully sifting through the distinctions, identifying all the changes that have taken place to cause the distinctions, or that have taken place within the distinctions.

A1. The young members of our church, ages 14-21, have stopped attending worship.

A2. No changes apparent.

A3. The young people no longer attend Sunday school.

B. No change apparent.

C1. No change apparent.

C2. About ten years ago the Sunday morning schedule was changed from:
—10:00 A.M. Sunday school classes, nursery through adult, and 11:00 A.M. worship for everyone

to the present schedule of:

—10:30 A.M. Sunday school for children, nursery through grade 8; morning worship for confirmees through adult.

PROBLEM ANALYSIS WORKSHEET

PROBLEM: Young people are not attending worship.

PRIORITY: Time: This is one of our most urgent
            Effect: problems, requiring immediate
            Trend: attention.

	What are the DIMENSIONS of the problem?		What is DISTINCTIVE between the two categories?	What CHANGES have occurred to cause this distinction?
	IS INVOLVED?	IS NOT INVOLVED?		
A. WHAT/WHO	Young members, age 14-21, do not attend worship services.	1. Two who do attend. 2. Young people over 21. 3. Youth under 14 do not attend Sunday school.	1. Not confirmed/members, just moved. 2. 3. Non-attenders used to attend S.S.	1. Young members don't attend church 2. 3. Y.P. over 14 don't attend S.S.
	DID/DOES IT OCCUR?	DID/DOES IT NOT OCCUR?		
B. WHERE	In Sunday morning worship services.	1. Sunday afternoon youth club. 2. Special worship events. 3. Other events.		
	DID/DOES IT OCCUR?	DID/DOES IT NOT OCCUR?		
C. WHEN	Don't know when first became serious. Has continued for a long time.	At other worship, social, and youth functions.	Occurs only at 10:30 A.M. Sunday worship, only activity concurrent with Sunday school hour.	Ten years ago schedule changed from 10 A.M. S.S. & 11 A.M. worship to 10:30 A.M. S.S. & worship concurrently.
	IS INVOLVED?	IS NOT INVOLVED?		
D. HOW MUCH/MANY (Extent)	22 members, ages 14-21, do not attend regularly.	Two young people do attend regularly.	Total membership, ages 14-21, involved, since two who attend regularly are not members.	These young people stopped attending church shortly after being confirmed.
POSSIBLE CAUSES: (* = most likely cause)			HOW CAN MOST LIKELY CAUSE BE TESTED?	

Steps in Problem Analysis	*Our Comments*

D. All these young people stopped attending worship sometime (we think shortly) after being confirmed.

STEP VI: Determine which change is the most likely cause of the problem and how this may be tested for validity.	This step actually involves three stages:
	1. Identifying all the changes that might possibly have caused the problem.
	2. Determining the one change that is most likely to be the cause.
	3. Testing the most likely cause to see whether it did in fact cause the problem.

Which of the changes might possibly have caused the problem?

1. Change A1 with distinction A1—possibly something about confirmation turned them against worship.
2. Change A1 with distinction A3—possibly the Sunday school failed to instruct them regarding the importance of worship.
3. Change C with distinction C—possibly when they were in Sunday

Any change, in order to qualify as a possible cause, must show a cause-and-effect relationship to one or more of the distinctions. Care must be given to search out all such relationships, as often the change and its cause-and-effect relationship to the problem may be so subtle and gradual that no one is aware of it.

As each possible cause is identified, it is stated in terms of a proposition to be tested.

PROBLEM ANALYSIS WORKSHEET

PROBLEM: Young people are not attending worship.

PRIORITY: Time: This is one of our most urgent.
Effect: problems, requiring immediate
Trend: attention.

	What are the DIMENSIONS of the problem?		What is DISTINCTIVE between the two categories?	What CHANGES have occurred to cause this distinction?
	IS INVOLVED?	IS NOT INVOLVED?		
A. WHAT/WHO	Young members, age 14-21, do not attend worship services.	1. Two who do attend. 2. Young people over 21. 3. Youth under 14 do not attend Sunday school.	1. Not confirmed/members, just moved. 2. 3. Non-attenders used to attend S.S.	1. Young members don't attend church. 2. 3. Y.P. over 14 don't attend S.S.
	DID/DOES IT OCCUR?	DID/DOES IT NOT OCCUR?		
B. WHERE	In Sunday morning worship services.	1. Sunday afternoon youth club. 2. Special worship events. 3. Other events.		
	DID/DOES IT OCCUR?	DID/DOES IT NOT OCCUR?		
C. WHEN	Don't know when first became serious. Has continued for a long time.	At other worship, social, and youth functions.	Occurs only at 10:30 A.M. Sunday worship, only activity concurrent with Sunday school hour.	Ten years ago schedule changed from 10 A.M. S.S. & 11 A.M. worship to 10:30 A.M. S.S. & worship concurrently.
	IS INVOLVED?	IS NOT INVOLVED?		
D. HOW MUCH/MANY (Extent)	22 members, ages 14-21, do not attend regularly.	Two young people do attend regularly.	Total membership, ages 14-21, involved, since two who attend regularly are not members.	These young people stopped attending church shortly after being confirmed.

POSSIBLE CAUSES: (* = most likely cause)	HOW CAN MOST LIKELY CAUSE BE TESTED?
1. Change A1 w/dist. A1—possibly confirmation turned them against worship.	1. Ask two who attend if they attended both as children.
2. Change A1 w/dist. A3—possibly S.S. failed to instruct them in importance of worship.	2. Check whether non-attenders now attend S.S. elsewhere.
3. Chance C w/dist. C—possibly when in S.S. they felt unwelcome in worship.	3. Ask them why they don't attend.
*4. Chance C w/dist. A3 & C—possibly new schedule conditioned them to believe S.S. is more important so when they couldn't attend S.S. they quit altogether.	

Steps in Problem Analysis

school they felt un-
wanted in worship.

4. Change C with distinc-
   tions A3 and C—
   possibly the change of
   schedule conditioned
   them, as children, to believe Sunday school was
   more important for them
   than worship. So when
   they could no longer go
   to Sunday school they
   just quit altogether.

Which of these combina-
tions would be MOST
LIKELY to cause the pro-
blem?

Change C with distinction
A3 and C.

The change of the schedule,
which made it impossible
for them, as children, to
attend both Sunday school
and worship, conditioned
them to believe that Sunday
school was more important.
So, when they reached the
age where a Sunday school
was no longer provided,
they quit going to church
altogether or began attending another church, where
there was a class available
to them.

*How can we test the most
likely cause to see whether it*

Our Comments

At this point all the changes
that have been listed as
possible causes are care-
fully analyzed to determine
which one would be most
likely to have caused the
problem. To qualify as the
most likely cause, the
change must explain the
distinction between the IS
and IS NOT characteristics
that are related to it. Would
this change likely produce
both sides of the
problem—the IS and the IS
NOT?

*At this stage the most likely
cause is treated as a proposi-*

Steps in Problem Analysis	*Our Comments*
will explain the distinction between the problem group and the non-problem group?	tion to be tested for validity. It is here where the group will often experience a potentially fatal temptation—to build a case in support of this change as the cause. This is no time to become nonanalytical! Instead, the likely cause should be subjected to a rigorous test to see whether it can stand as the most likely cause.
A. Ask the two who attend if they grew up attending both Sunday school and worship. B. Check to see whether any of the non-attenders are attending Sunday school elsewhere. C. Ask them why they don't attend.	This test of the change that seems most likely to have caused the problem is carried out against the facts established in Step III. In order to qualify as the most likely cause, the change must support, without exception or assumption, all the facts identified in Step III and the relevant distinctions in Step IV. If the most likely cause selected first does not hold up under such scrutiny, it is abandoned in search for another most likely cause, or more work is done to further clarify the dimensions of the problem.

TESTING THE MOST LIKELY CAUSE

A visit with the two young people who were attending indicated they had grown up in a church and a family where it was expected that everyone attend both Sunday school and worship. They were disappointed to discover Christ Church did not have classes for young people and were planning to seek out another church where there were such classes.

A visit or telephone call to each of the non-attenders uncovered the fact that several were attending classes and worship either in other churches or at a local Christian coffeehouse. During the same visit, each was asked why he or she did not attend worship at Christ Church. Some of the older ones indicated they remembered the squabble ten years previous when the schedule was changed because some influential persons did not want children in worship services, and having attended worship themselves when they were children, they now wanted their own children to attend with them. Since this was not possible at Christ Church, they were attending elsewhere.

Several of the younger ones indicated their feelings of confusion during their years in the Sunday school when the teachers stressed the importance of worship but they could not worship with their parents. If it was really important, they had reasoned, why couldn't they do it? Having not attended when they were young, they just "sorta never developed the habit," so when there was no longer a class for them to attend they had lost interest.

When this information was reported to the administrative board early in January, they were indeed convinced their analysis had led them to the most likely cause. But the story is not over. The results of the action they took to correct the problem were certainly as dramatic as the problem itself. They immediately arranged a meeting with the Christian education committee, during which it was decided that a schedule of Sunday services would be developed that would encourage and allow persons of all ages to attend Sunday classes and worship. The congregation would be allowed to experience the new schedule for three months before being asked to approve or disapprove it.

The decision was implemented as follows:

1. Throughout February the new schedule and the reasoning behind it were interpreted to the membership.
2. The new schedule was followed March through May:
   10:00 A.M.—Worship services for the entire family
   10:45 A.M.—Coffee and Coke break
   11:00 A.M.—Classes for all ages
   11:45 A.M.—Dismissal
3. New classes added were:
   a. High school
   b. College and career
   c. Adult Bible study
   d. Adult discussion of Christianity and current events
   The average attendance at the new classes during the quarter were: high school, eight; college and career, ten; adult Bible study, fifteen; adult discussion, eight. The attendance at worship also experienced a dramatic increase owing to the presence of children and youth. Two new families began attending when they learned children were welcome. Not all was roses, however. Two older couples left the church, complaining about the disturbance of children in the worship, as did a young mother, complaining she could not get anyting out of worship when she had to worry about her children squirming and making noise.
4. At a special meeting in June, the results were reported to the congregation, which was then asked to approve or disapprove the schedule for the coming fall. The congregation approved.
5. The following September it became the official schedule, enjoying the same results.

Perhaps we cannot always expect such dramatic results simply because we use systems problem-solving approaches. Their experience, however, does underscore some important considerations:

1. It is unlikely they would have experienced similar results by taking action on any of the earlier suggested causes: "Young people just aren't interested in church

124

and religion nowadays," "I think we've got to get to the parents," "Maybe we need a special service for them," "I think we just have to expect it to be this way."

2. Without a systems approach, it is unlikely they ever would have discovered the cause—a schedule change made ten years earlier and now accepted as routine and right.

3. The problem analysis took a couple of hours—a precious amount of time, to be sure. But, in terms of identifying and solving the problem, this was time well spent.

When Problems Are a Real Mess

Ever hear someone exclaim, "This situation is a real mess"? A mess results from several problems, each arising from its own distinct cause, becoming all tangled together so that one cannot seem to make heads or tails of any of them.

Unless the problems in a mess are taken apart and

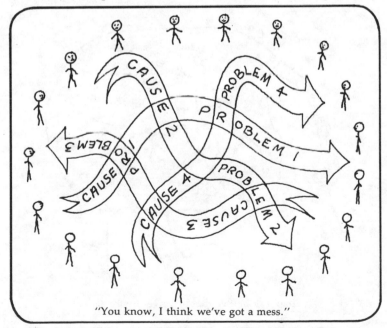

"You know, I think we've got a mess."

specifically analyzed one by one, the mess may continue to thwart all problem-solving efforts for years.

Actually, the Christ Church case, complex as it was, was not too difficult to analyze, even though the change that effected the cause had occurred ten years before. The search for cause was greatly facilitated by the fact that the problem and its cause had not become entangled with a host of other problems. That would have been a real mess!

Where Problems Cause Other Problems: Cause-and-Effect Chain

Contrary to a mess, in which problems have distinct causes but do not become entangled, there are those situations where a problem itself becomes the cause of another problem, thus creating a cause-and-effect chain of problems. In a mess there are as many distinct causes as there are problems. In a cause-and-effect chain of problems

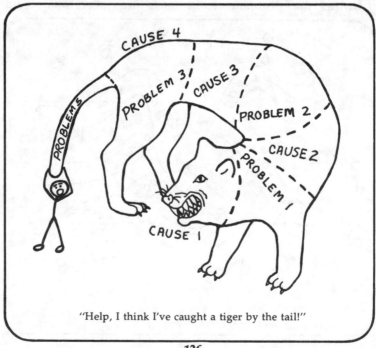

"Help, I think I've caught a tiger by the tail!"

there is one underlying cause to all the problems, which are related to it in a sequential fashion.

In such cases problem analysis is essential. A chain of problems can satisfactorily be dealt with only in a manner that allows the problem solver to identify the cause-and-effect relationships within the system.

Applying the Process

Problem analysis is based upon the concept that at the root of every problem is a change in one of the distinctive features or processes in the system. Thus problem analysis is a search for those changes which are most influential in hindering the church from achieving its mission and objectives. Without that knowledge the church will accomplish its mission only by accident.

Problem analysis is a flexible process, not a rigid program. It does not have to be applied exactly as it was described here. Fortunately, a great many problems can be sufficiently analyzed in a few minutes to suggest the most likely cause and point to a possible solution. Simply asking the *WHAT, WHEN,* and *WHERE* questions to establish the problem's dimensions is often sufficient analysis. The key to practicality and success is to do no more analysis than is necessary to identify the most likely cause, but always to do a thorough enough analysis to assure that the group does not jump to conclusions, assuming a cause and then proceeding to build a case to support their assumptions.

Perhaps it would be helpful to illustrate how the use of the dimensions questions alone can sometimes point to the causes of a problem.

Community Church

The district superintendent was able to help the Community Church board (chapter 3, pp. 29-32) quickly develop a list of possible causes of their financial problems, and to select the most likely cause from that list by suggesting that their problem had a basic cause and then asking one question: *"What* do you think the cause of this problem might be?" One might have suspected they would have decided the poor organization of the pledge campaign was the cause. No doubt this was a contributing factor. They decided, however, that the cause lay deeper than the organization of the pledge campaign. The member who said the church had no purpose or mission and perhaps should close its doors was voicing the sentiments of others in that meeting and throughout the congregation.

Environmental Change

The administrative board of a congregation located on the edge of a giant metropolitan area was kept from jumping to a potentially serious conclusion by one analytical question. The denomination had opened the mission church after receiving several inquires from members of the denomination who had recently moved out of the city to a rapidly expanding suburb that was literally pushing its way into the cornfields. When the congregation was established, several farm families took membership there, and the administrative board had a balance of suburban and farm representation. This case began when the board launched a stewardship campaign to "increase the annual income from the congregation by 25 percent in the next two years." The contributions during the first year of the campaign, however, remained about the same as the previous year in spite of the stewardship emphasis. The board concluded their campaign had been a failure and called upon us to help them plan a more effective stewardship approach. It seemed apparent to us that the enthusiasm of the congregation was at a high point. But, we also concluded, there might be some distinct differences between the suburbanites and the farm families—distinctions about which they might not be aware, and which may have had some influence on the congregation's giving.

We asked whether any changes in either group's ability to support the church might have occurred unnoticed by the total group. After awhile a suburbanite said, "Well, I don't know how much it hurt us, but when X Company transferred their plant some of our suburban members had a rough time for awhile." Then a farmer said, "Last year we lost a lot of our crop because of drought. This has affected our giving this year." A quick check with other churches in nearby communities indicated the per member giving of this church was significantly above what other churches had enjoyed over the year. The board concluded that the cause for not reaching the goal in increased contributions was an adverse shift in the economic conditions of several of the member families. They also concluded that their stewardship campaign had been a success, which they reported to the congregation with a service of celebration.

CONCLUSION
Change is unavoidable and constant, and problems in the church are usually not an indication of a lack of spirituality or of sin in the camp. Any church that is intentional about its mission will experience deviations from its desired results.

Unplanned change is usually in a negative direction. Murphy's Law declares: "If any thing can possibly go wrong, it will." Therefore, a church left to itself will tend to become more and more irrelevant as the changes occurring without and within steer it further and further away from its mission.

At this point we wish to remind you that the Church is a uniquely spiritual institution and, as such, often confronts problems of a uniquely spiritual nature. Paul said, "For our fight is not against human foes, but against cosmic powers, against the authorities and potentates of this dark world, against the superhuman forces of evil in the heavens" (Eph. 6:12 NEB). The apostles encountered certain problems in their ministry that Jesus said would yield only to prayer (Matt. 17:21). This holds true for the Church today. In the midst of applying the effective organizational methodologies at his or her disposal today, the spiritually sensitive and professionally competent pastor will recognize the difference between those problems which spring from organizational deficiencies and are amenable to organizational processes, and those which are of supernatural origins and can be solved only by leading the congregation to its knees in prayer and reliance upon God. Even as we become more and more skilled, let us not forget that the Church still finds the solutions to its greatest problems on its knees. The methodologies that we are here discussing are no substitute for prayer, fasting, and faith.

> *If anything can possibly go wrong, it will.*
> Murphy's Law

CHAPTER 8
Decision Analysis

Fortune is the ruler of half our activities, but she allows the other half, or thereabouts, to be ruled by us.

Niccolò Machiavelli

DECISION ANALYSIS: What to Do When a Course of Action Is Not Readily Apparent

The problem analysis detailed in the preceeding chapter leads to a decision about the most likely cause of the problem, Step 6 on the problem analysis model, p. 106. This is a decision *not* about how the problem may be solved, but only about the problem's cause.

Fortunately a good problem analysis will often indicate possible solutions. Occasionally, however, the problem is of such a nature that knowing its most likely cause does little to suggest the course of action most likely to solve the problem. When this is the case, you will want to follow the problem analysis with a decision analysis—a systems approach to select the most favorable course of action from among alternatives (Step 7 on the model shown on page 106).

There are other compelling reasons for conducting a decision analysis. It is a rare problem that can be solved in only one way. For most problems, there are many alternate solutions, and the wise problem solver will no sooner jump to conclusions about the most effective solution than he or she will make hasty assumptions about the cause of the problem. Therefore, after the problem analysis, it will often be necessary to conduct a decision analysis to identify several possible courses of action and to determine the one most likely to succeed.

Many decision analyses can be conducted in a few minutes; others will need to be very thoroughly done in order to get at all the information needed to formulate action alternatives. On page 133 is a model for a decision analysis. This model is an explication of Step 7 of the model on page 106. You will note that it begins where the problem analysis leaves off, with a description of the cause of the problem.[1]

Imposing this decision analysis model upon a problem in order to select a solution would require something like the following analysis.

1. Problem and Cause Formulation
   a. How well can we describe the problem to be solved?
   b. What is the most likely cause of this problem?
   c. What are the theological-missional, organizational, and interpersonal aspects of this problem?
   d. In which system component does this problem lie?
2. Objectives
   a. What do we want to accomplish in solving this problem?
   b. What are the specific issues that need to be confronted in meeting these objectives?
   c. If these issues are resolved, will we know the problem has been solved?
      1) If *no*, continue working on problem formulation and objectives.
      2) If *yes*, proceed with analysis.
3. Resources and Constraints
   a. What is there in each component of the church system that will act as a resource or constraint to meeting each of the objectives?
   b. Can the constraints be reduced? How?
   c. What time, facilities, and people are available for achieving the objectives?

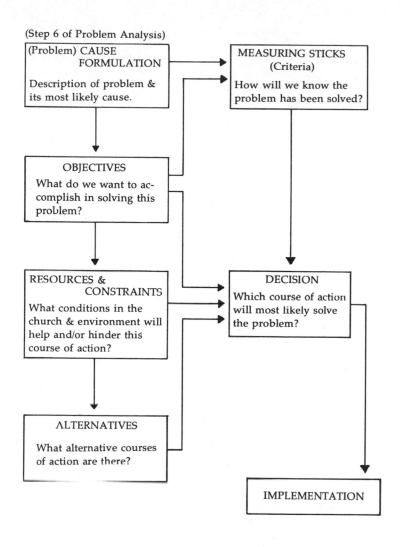

(Problem) CAUSE
FORMULATION

Description of problem &
its most likely cause.

MEASURING STICKS
(Criteria)

How will we know the
problem has been solved?

OBJECTIVES

What do we want to ac-
complish in solving this
problem?

RESOURCES &
CONSTRAINTS

What conditions in the
church & environment will
help and/or hinder this
course of action?

DECISION

Which course of action
will most likely solve
the problem?

ALTERNATIVES

What alternative courses
of action are there?

IMPLEMENTATION

A DECISION ANALYSIS MODEL

    d. What is there in the church's environment that will act as resources or constraints?

4. Criteria
   a. How will we know when the problem has been solved? What will be different?
   b. How will we measure the degree to which our objectives have been met and the problem has been solved?
   c. What are the requirements of a good set of decisions to solve this problem?
   d. When will each of these decisions be needed, and by whom?

5. Decision
   a. What course of action will most likely solve the problem?
   b. What will the result of these decisions look like?
   c. How will we evaluate our problem-solving effort?

6. Alternatives
   a. If this course of action for solving the problem should prove unsatisfactory, what are the alternatives?

7. Implementation
   a. Who is the person or group who needs to approve this plan before it can become functional?
   b. How should the plan be implemented? When? By whom?

Imposing the decision analysis model upon a problem to decide upon a possible solution may take only a few minutes for a simple problem, or it may take several hours or days when you are confronting a very complex problem.

> *The first principle of composition, then, is to foresee or determine the shape of what is to come, and to pursue that shape.*
> William Strunk, Jr.

CHAPTER 9

The Pastor as Church Manager

If God has given you . . . administrative ability, take the responsibility seriously.
Romans 12:8 (TLB)

We turn now to examine the role of the pastor as church manager. We are aware that for various reasons many pastors shy away from administrative or managerial tasks. However, like pregnancy, administrative concerns will not go away even if no attention is given to them. Consciously or unconsciously, a church will move in some direction, make decisions, and carry out programs. We strongly urge that the role of pastor-as-manager or administrator be intentionally assumed, its needed skills be acquired, and its functions performed effectively.

Throughout this book we have set forth a systems approach to church management. The pastor must become the channel through whom this approach is initiated and utilized in the life of the local church because of the very nature of the office of pastor. In this chapter we are seeking to provide help for readers who want assistance in assuming the role of pastor-as-manager.

PERSPECTIVE

The study of organizational design and management is something we have given very little time to in the Church. Except for periodic reform movements, Church structures were accepted as part of Church tradition. However, institutions and structures that stood unchallenged for generations prior to the 1960s have within the past fifteen years been forced to undertake radical change or be rejected by the very people they were intended to serve. During these years some predicted the Church would not or could not meet such demands for change, and that it would wither and die. The Church did meet these demands, however, and continues to make effective changes in many areas of its life. The area in which it has found change to be most difficult is the area that it has studied the least—organizational design and management. By and large we are structural fundamentalists in regard to our organizational structures. And yet, those structures which were initiated by the Church in a drastically different setting need now to be scrutinized and, we suspect, in some cases given up in favor of structures more appropriate to the Church in its new environment.

God has revealed to us his nature and his mission of redemptive love. He has not, however, told us *how* to organize and manage the Church as it engages in this mission. These structures and processes are in need of constant alteration and renewal in response to changing circumstances and environment.

It is important to recognize that the Church has never developed a uniquely ecclesiastical organizational structure, but has always borrowed its organizational structures, and resulting management styles, from its secular environment. Therefore, there is nothing divine or uniquely religious about any of the structures we now have. The Church's borrowing from its secular environment is somewhat understandable. Since it shares with secular organizations many elements of its environment, it has assumed that procedures that are effective in secular organizations would also be

136

effective in religious organizations. It is not quite this simple.

Adopting procedures that are effective in secular organizations is often the wrong prescription for religious organizations. The Church has a totally unique mission to perform, and persons join its ranks for unique and special reasons. This uniqueness of mission and membership requires the Church critically to examine secular organization design and procedure before adapting it for its purposes. When and if adapted, such procedures need to be made subservient to the mission they are intended to facilitate. Since they are not divine, however, the organizational procedures used by the Church need to be just as critically scrutinized *after* they are adopted as before. The proper rule for the Church today is not "Whatever we do today, we'll do forever," but "Whatever we do today will in all likelihood be a candidate for abandonment within a fairly short period of years."

Moving from an encapsulated perspective on the Church in relation to ecclesiastical management, we now move to the local scene to put into perspective the pastor's relationship to local church management.

Throughout this book we have taken a wholistic view of the pastor's role, characterizing it as involving prophetic, priestly, and kingly functions. Many pastors, as evidenced in various research projects, enjoy the prophetic and priestly roles and feel better prepared to function in them than they do in the kingly, or managerial, roles. One reason for this may be they have not been as well prepared to be administrators and managers as they have to be priests and prophets. Another reason often cited is that the priestly and prophetic roles are perceived as being more central to the core of the gospel, and their calling. Actually, a balanced ministry requires that *each* be emphasized. Moreover, the Christian community must give attention to organization and structure in order to minister to its own members, as well as to express its mission or witness to the world.

Properly understood, a systems approach to church

management emphasizes the interrelationship of the prophetic (mission) and priestly (personal) roles with the kingly (managerial) role. We have chosen to focus on the managerial role, hoping to provide assistance to pastors and laity in church leadership positions who are seeking help in this area. The practice of ministry, indeed, requires unending attention to prophetic, priestly, and kingly functions and their interrelationship.

THE DIMENSIONS OF MANAGEMENT

The word *management* has various connotations for different persons. Some feel it implies a manipulative, bureaucratic, business-focused concept and prefer the word *administration*. Others reject the word *administration* as connoting the performing of executive functions and chores. For these reasons we feel it necessary to define the word *management* as we are using it in relation to the church and the pastor's role.

Management involves the work of the clergy and lay officials, including all functions of enabling the church to establish its mission and facilitate movement toward it. It involves the function of providing spiritual and organizational leadership to the church system or subsystem for which the person is responsible. This definition of church management is quite similar to Lindgren's more detailed definition of church administration in *Foundations for Purposeful Church Administration.*[1]

The pastor must always keep the kingly, or management, role in perspective in relation to the prophetic and priestly roles. He or she must also be careful not to place too high a value on the church as an institution. Peter Drucker, one of the foremost authorities and writers in the field of management, pointedly challenges managers to keep in focus their view of institutions. "They [institutions] are not ends in themselves, but means. The right question to ask in respect to them is not, 'What are they?' but, 'What are they supposed to be doing and what are their tasks?'"[2] Drucker goes on to remind management that it has no independent or autonomous existence within the institution. Management is simply a component within the organization charged with the responsibility of enabling all the resources and functions of the organization to be utilized in establishing its mission and facilitating movement toward it.

THE TASKS OF MANAGEMENT

We believe the three tasks of management as set forth by Drucker are right on target for church management. The three tasks which management has to perform to enable the institution to function are:

"1. Clarifying the specific purpose and mission of the institution.
2. Making work productive, and the worker achieving.
3. Managing social impacts and social responsibilities."[3]

What would these three tasks mean to the pastor assuming the role of church manager? These three tasks become *top priority guidelines* in terms of managerial functioning. They answer the question, What is a manager supposed to do?

As manager, the pastor is to assume responsibility for keeping purpose and mission in the forefront of all activities—*i.e.*, goal-setting, planning, programming, and evaluating. He or she is to seek to establish conditions that are conducive to making all of the energy and work that persons expend in the church productive in facilitating the church's mission (and not time-wasting busy work).

The most valuable resource of any church is its human resources. Therefore, as a second responsibility the pastor-as-manager must see persons as such, and seek to have their involvement be fruitful not only in accomplishing the church's mission but in contributing to their personal growth and achievement. Placing a high value on the worth and growth of the person is becoming more and more important in our society for all institutions. Church managers, in their zeal for carrying out programs, must not exploit persons. Consideration for human beings *and* the church's mission must go hand in hand.

The third managerial task requiring continual attention is the social impacts and responsibilities of the Church. An institution exists not in a vacuum, but in relation to other institutions and to society. The Church must, therefore, always act responsibly in relation to all persons and institutions. This requires a conscious attention to minister to institutions as well as to persons. The pastor's task, as church manager, is to enable his or her church to perceive its programs and activities in relation to how they affect society.

These, then, are the three main tasks of the pastor as church manager:

1. To clarify the specific purpose and mission of the church.
2. To involve persons in ways that will facilitate mission *and* promote personal growth.
3. To consider the social impacts and responsibilities of church actions.

WHY A SYSTEMS APPROACH TO CHURCH MANAGEMENT?

Up to this point we have set forth the dimensions of management and what the main management tasks are. Further, we have illustrated these aspects of management in relation to the pastor's role as church manager. We now propose to indicate how a systems view of organizations provides the pastor with the resources needed to assume the role of church manager.

In chapter 2 we discussed five types of organizational structures and polities being used by church leaders today: traditional, charismatic, classical, human relations, and systems. Each of these organizational styles, you will recall, places its own unique emphasis upon the growth and goal achievement of the organization and upon the growth and goal achievement of individuals within the organization. Pastors who place higher emphasis upon the growth and goal achievement of the organization prefer traditional, charismatic, or classical structures; while those who place higher emphasis upon the growth and goal achievement of individuals prefer human relations structures. The pastor, however, who places equal emphasis upon the growth and goal achievement of the organization and upon the growth and goal achievement of its individual members will prefer the systems approach. There may well be those situations in which, for reasons beyond his or her control, one must model an organization after one of the other organizational styles. The pastor need not be content with this style of organization, however, and can consistently seek to move the church toward a systems approach.

A systems approach to church management does not promise to be simple, and requires great leadership skill. Indeed, a primary commitment to both the concerns of the organization and to those of individuals can be expected to require more time for making decisions, living with many different goals, openness in dealing with conflict, and greater communication skills than would be needed by pastors using any other organizational approach. But while a systems approach to ministry does not promise to be any easier, it does promise to be more effective in those situations where the pastor is concerned to see both the organization *and* its members experience growth and goal achievement, and where changes in the church and its environment threaten the effectiveness of its programs.

The possibility for increased effectiveness through a systems approach is due in part to several systems management tools. Each organizational theory calls for a particular management style in which certain techniques become acceptable and appropriate. These same techniques would, of course, be unacceptable and inappropriate in organizations based upon a different theory. In this book we have discussed four systems management tools: developing missional intentionality, relating the church and environment, program planning and budgeting, and problem analysis. We chose these as illustrative of the application of systems theory to organizational issues. Since these management tools are based upon systems theory, they exhibit many of the same concepts and characteristics as the theory itself. For example, each of these tools:

1. Is comprised of a set of *coordinated components* working together to accomplish a common objective.
2. Is focused toward clarifying and/or achieving the *mission* and *goals* of the church while at the same time clarifying and enhancing the quality of human relationships and personal achievement.
3. Is extremely effective in providing the church system with useful *information* for decision-making about itself and its environment.
4. Enables the church to identify *environmental conditions* that are affecting its programs and to remain relevant by making appropriate *responses.*
5. Greatly facilitate *communications* between individuals and groups in the system.
6. Is adaptable to fit the needs of the system.

The systems approach should be effective in the local church because it provides the concepts and tools for zeroing in on the two most intangible realities of the church's organizational life—its mission and its environment—with clearly defined and measurable goals and plans. And, systems theory seeks to do this in such a way that the entire congregation will be motivated to achieve the goals.

The classical, traditional, and charismatic theories stress organizational goals and growth as the polar region of management effectiveness. The human relations theory stresses the goals and growth of individuals as the polar region of management effectiveness. To plant both your feet in either camp is to create for yourself and your church an organizational polarization, a ministerial imbalance. We believe the systems theory of organizations offers a balanced and effective context for church managers.

THE PASTOR AS CHURCH MANAGER

The goal of this chapter is to help the pastor try on the role of a church manager within a systems framework:

—To understand the objectives of a systems church manager.
—To discover what this role would involve.
—To find out what skills would be needed.

THE PASTOR'S OBJECTIVES AS CHURCH MANAGER

The pastor who accepts the role of a church manager within the context of a systems understanding of organizations will be committed to the objective of making the local church, in Drucker's words, "a true whole that is larger than the sum of its parts." He or she will seek to take a wholistic view of the church with the help of systems theory. The interaction and relationship of each of the subsystems to another and to the whole will be kept in focus by a clear view of mission—the end reason for being. The pastor will be much like the conductor of a symphony orchestra, or a football coach, whose ability to enhance the performance of each individual will bring forth a total performance much greater than the sum of the parts. The pastor will seek to make the witness and acts of the Christian community (local church) much more than the sum of individual members or sub-church groups. A systems theory of organizations will provide the tools and means for achieving such a wholistic gestalting of the church's life and witness.

The second objective of such a pastor is always to be aware of both the immediate and long-range effects of all decisions. As Drucker points out so clearly, if there is no next hundred days, there will be no next hundred years. It is indeed difficult to keep your nose to the grindstone and lift your eyes to the hills at the same time. Systems concepts provide tools to enable the pastor to evaluate the effect of alternative decisions and actions so that difficult decisions can be made. Systems theory's continuous concern for the changing environment corroborates this objective of keeping in focus the importance of both the immediate and long-range futures.

WORK AREA RESPONSIBILITIES
OF A CHURCH MANAGER

Within the framework of these two prime objectives of the pastor's role as church manager there are six work-area responsibilities:

1. Clarifying mission and setting of objectives.
2. Planning and integrating.
3. Organizing and designing structures.
4. Motivating and communicating.
5. Evaluating.
6. Stimulating personal growth of self and others.[4]

Each of the above will be discussed very briefly to illustrate what is involved in each area.

Clarifying Mission and Setting Objectives

The pastor, as part of his or her managerial role, has a responsibility for developing a clear understanding of mission on the part of the church. A systems approach would require congregational participation in that process as well as in setting specific objectives to accomplish the mission. Goals with specific, realizable, measurable objectives must be developed from the church's understanding of its mission.

Planning and Integrating

Action plans must be forthcoming from objectives, or planning will be only a paper activity. The respective plans of the many subgroups in a church must be coordinated and integrated on *all* levels—*e.g.,* movement toward mission, use of personnel, scheduling, financing, interaction with other church groups, the whole church, and the church's impact on the community.

Organizing and Designing Structures

Decisions regarding *who, what, when,* and *how* all have to be made in regard to church programs. Manageable structures and groups need to be evolved for each task. These structures must both facilitate the task and stimulate growth of the participants.

Motivating and Communicating

Persons must be motivated to become involved. The earlier in the process persons become involved, the more likely they will be motivated to participate to the end. The manager is concerned about making a team out of the participants. His or her personal relationship with team members and the functioning process used in the group contribute much to the open communication necessary within groups and between groups.

Evaluating

The pastor's role as manager requires that a specific process of measuring the effectiveness of what is happening in relation to the church's mission be established. Clear yardsticks must be adopted for evaluation of performance. Participants must be involved in the evaluations. Evaluations must then be used to design future programs.

Stimulating Future Growth in Self and Others

Human resources are the church's greatest asset. God has revealed himself through persons from the beginning of time. The pastor as manager must seek to provide experiences and relationships in the church and its programs that will be challenging, growth producing, and maturing in personal as well as spiritual dimensions.

CONCLUSION

The pastor who is ready to accept his or her role as a church manager must make a commitment to secure the competencies required for an acceptable performance of the role. This commitment will need to be a long-term involvement including a willingness to do reading in the field, to experiment in the local church, to take training in related areas, and to seek opportunities to share common concerns with other clergy and laity as well.

In this book we have limited our presentation to systems theory and church management from an organizational point of view. These same areas need to be studied from the point of view of human dynamics and motivation and from the perspective of developing specific skills in such areas as decision-making, leadership styles, dealing with conflict, and so forth. These topics remain for another book, which the authors hope to publish in the near future, dealing with organizational development and church management.

> *To be a manager requires more than a title, a big office, and other outward symbols of rank. It requires competence and performance of a high order.*
>
> Peter Drucker

Notes

Chapter 1. A Balanced Ministry for Today's Church

1. We do not know for certain how long it took Noah to build the ark, although *Zondervan Pictorial Bible Dictionary* states it took 120 years. See Merrill C. Tenney, ed., *Zondervan Pictorial Bible Dictionary* (Grand Rapids: Zondervan, 1967), p. 589.

2. For a recent statement on Worley's views on the local church, see Robert C. Worley, *A Gathering of Strangers: Understanding the Life of Your Congregation.*

3. John Calvin, *Institutes of the Christian Religion,* trans. John Allen, Book II, Ch. XV (Grand Rapids: Eerdmans, 1949), pp. 540-50.

4. Robert C. Worley, "The King Is Dead: An Inquiry into Wise Rule in the Church," a paper delivered at the Conference on the Ministry in the 70's, February 8–9, 1971.

Chapter 2. The Influence of Organization Theory on the Practice of Ministry.

1. We shall discuss in greater detail the styles of leadership utilized by church leaders, and the effects of these styles, in a later companion volume.

2. The charismatic theory of organization is not to be confused with the style of religious expression commonly called the Charismatic Movement or Charismatic Experience. The charismatic theory of organization is practiced in nonreligious as well as religious organizations.

3. For a detailed application of each of these five theories to the church, see Peter Rudge, *Ministry and Management.*

4. For example, the Catholic Church, with one person sitting at the top of its worldwide operation, is often identified as the purest historical example of the classical theory. The United Methodist Church, however, has not one person at the top but a number of bishops, each with equal status and authority. The United Methodist Church, then, is a variation of the pure classical model. Some of the larger churches and their most famous pastors in The United Methodist Church, however, have at times espoused the charismatic leader theory—*e.g.,* Ernest Fremont Tittle at First Church, Evanston. For those of you who may not know, Ernest Fremont Tittle was, in the 1920s and 1930s, a great charismatic proponent of the social gospel. In contrast to this, much of the social activism in local United Methodist churches in the 1960s was organized upon the human relations theory.

Chapter 3. Viewing the Church from a Systems Perspective

1. There are many systems and systems theories, such as biological, social, astrological, and so forth. In this book we are talking only about organizational systems, although much systems theory is applicable to all types of systems.

2. The term *transforming* is not to be taken here in a theological sense. All systems have a transforming process, as described in the text.

3. For a discussion of the impact of environment upon a system, see E. J. Miller and A. K. Rice, *Systems of Organization* (London: Tavistock Publications, 1967). Also see John Maurer, ed., *Readings in Organizational Theory: Open Systems Approaches* (New York: Random House, 1971).

4. A word of caution needs to be given here. The temptation to stall decision-making in order to gather more information needs to be balanced by the need for decisions to be made in order for work to get done. There comes a point in church planning when decisions must be made in spite of lack of data. This situation is made more tolerable to the persons involved if they know what is happening, and that the structure resulting from the decisions will not be carved in stone but will remain open to evaluation and alteration as new and more effective information is gathered. What is more intolerable is to make a bad decision or to create an ineffective structure and then to stick to it, come hell or high water.

Chapter 4. Mission Intentionality and Systems Theory

1. George S. Odiorne, *Management and the Activity Trap.*

2. The following resources will be helpful to those interested in pursuing a study of the nature and mission of the church:

Ernest Best, *One Body in Christ* (London: S.P.C.K., 1955).

Robert McAfee Brown, *The Significance of the Church* (Philadelphia: Westminster Press, 1956).

Howard Grimes, *The Church Redemptive* (Nashville: Abindgon, 1958).

James M. Gustafson, *Treasure in Earthen Vessels: The Church as a Human Community* (New York: Harper, 1961).

Donald G. Miller, *The Nature and Mission of the Church* (Richmond: John Knox Press, 1957).

Paul Minear, *Images of the Church in the New Testament* (Westminster Press, 1960).

H. Richard Niebuhr, *The Purpose of the Church and Its Ministry* (Harper, 1956).

Alan Richardson, *An Introduction to the Theology of the New Testament* (Harper, 1959).

D. Elton Trueblood, *The Company of the Committed* (Harper, 1961).

Hans Kung, *The Church* (New York: Sheed & Ward, 1967), and *Truthfulness, the Future of the Church* (Sneed & Ward, 1968).

Richard P. McBrien, *The Remaking of the Church* (Harper, 1973).

3. Kung, *The Church*.

4. Minear, *Images of the Church in the New Testament*.

Chapter 5. Interaction of Church and Environment

1. Robert E. Corrigan and Roger A. Kaufman, *Why Systems Engineering* (Palo Alto: Fearon Publishers, 1966).

2. *Interface* is a systems term referring to the point of interaction or contact between two systems, subsystems, groups, or persons.

3. Richard J. C. Roeber, *The Organization in a Changing Environment* (Reading, Mass.: Addison-Wesley Publishing Company, 1973), p. 155.

4. Paul R. Lawrence and Jay Lorsch, *Organization and Environment* (Homewood, Ill.: Richard D. Irwin, 1969), p. 14.

5. Robert B. Duncan, a paper entitled *Multiple Decision Making Structures in Adapting to Environmental Uncertainty* (Evanston, Ill.: Northwestern University, 1973).

6. The concept of a "linking person" was originated by Rensis Likert to apply to representatives of various subsystems in the organizational structure, but could apply equally well here. See Rensis Likert, *The Human Organization: Its Management and Value* (New York: McGraw-Hill, 1967).

7. Roeber, *The Organization in a Changing Environment*.

Chapter 6. Program Planning and Budgeting System

1. For an entire book devoted to this subject see Charles Kepner and Benjamin Tregoe, *The Rational Manager: A Systematic Approach to Problem Solving and Decision Making*.

2. See chapter 3 for a detailed definition of a system.

3. See chapter 3 for a description of the components and a discussion of their interrelatedness.

4. See chapter 4 for details of developing a congregation's mission statement.

5. PPBS, as a management system, formulates programs, plans, and budgets at every level of the church system; starting at the bottom and moving toward the top of the organizational hierarchy. This is, of course, a radically different approach to decision-making than the charismatic, traditional, or classical management approaches, in which decisions and plans are determined at the top and fed downward throughout the church.

6. PPBS is a process, not a tightly structured program. The flow of activities, time-line, and the processes utilized can, and should, be modified to best suit the size, needs, and abilities of the congregation. The flow chart presented here is for purposes of illustration only.

7. The dates given here are for purposes of illustrating a possible PPBS calendar, and would need to be adjusted to suit the church's needs.

8. Chapter 4 describes a process for developing a mission statement. For assistance in conducting congregational self-assessment processes, see Robert C. Worley, *Dry Bones Breathe* (Philadelphia: Westminster Press, 1977), and Norman Shawchuck and Richard A. Miller, *Guide to Self-Assessment and Mission* (Bloomington, Minn.: The Synod of Lakes and Prairies, The United Presbyterian Church, USA, January, 1976).

9. For a helpful discussion of structuring a system along programmatic lines see chapter 6, "Program Budgeting," in C. West Churchman *The Systems Approach*.

10. There are many resources available to assist in the goal-setting and planning process, such as: Edward Dayton's workbook *God's Purpose/Man's Plans* (Monrovia, Cal.: World Vision International); Don Mills' workbook *Let's Plan* (Ontario: United Church of Canada Distribution Center); and Shawchuck, Worley, Lewis, and Gray, *Experiences in Activating Congregations*.

11. For a delightful and imaginative description of reallocation and of constructing a program budget see Lyle Schaller "Put Your Budget to Work," *The Lutheran*, November 8, 1967.

12. For a planning model only, you may use all the concepts and methods set forth in this chapter, excluding the processes that pertain to budgeting. For those churches which traditionally have operated without a budget and budget approval, this may be necessary.

We really hope you will use PPBS, but we wouldn't want to fool you. PPBS is a sophisticated concept and, as you know, the way most churches prepare the budget is a very unsophisticated process. To install a PPBS in your church will take time and energy. Maybe you will want to start on a limited scale by having two or three program committees experiment with the process the first year, phase in more committees the second year, and get the entire church involved the third year.

Chapter 7. Problem Analysis

1. These two concepts, first suggested by Herbert Simon in 1960, have become the foundational premises of most effective systems problem-solving approaches. See Herbert Simon, *The New Science of Management Decision* (New York: Harper, 1960).

2. The search for cause, while essential to problem solving, has immobilized more than one church or pastor who spends too much time attempting to reconstruct events of the past rather than shaping events in the future. Odiorne declares "The only practical justification for finding causes is to solve a problem or to assure a better future. When the search for causes reverts to picking over the rubbish heap of past events for scandals and scapegoats, it is unworthy and unproductive work." He then discusses nine possible fallacies in relating cause and effect which you may find helpful and interesting. George Odiorne, *Management and the Activity Trap.*

3. An entire book has been given over to this sequence of steps in problem analysis and should be read by anyone responsible for solving organizational problems: Charles Kepner and Benjamin Tregoe, *The Rational Manager: A Systematic Approach to Problem Solving and Decision Making.*

4. Kepner and Tregoe have included illustrations of many helpful problem and decision analysis instruments in their book.

Chapter 8. Decision Analysis

1. In their book *The Rational Manager,* Kepner and Tregoe present a format for decision analysis that is different from the one presented here. There are many others. The important thing is to use an approach that assures action plans are arrived at logically and systematically, and not based upon wild guesswork and assumptions.

Chapter 9. The Pastor as Church Manager

1. Alvin J. Lindgren, *Foundations for Purposeful Church Administration.*

2. Peter F. Drucker, *Management: Tasks, Responsibilities, Practices.*

3. *Ibid.,* p. 40.

4. This list is quite similar to Lindgren's "administrative

process" discussed in an earlier volume, *Foundations for Purposeful Church Administration*, pp. 69-84. The list is also very similar to a list by Drucker in *Management*, pp. 399-405. Most writers on management include these items in some form as basic work responsibilities of managers.

Bibliography

There is at present a proliferation of publications dealing with systems theory. Following is a brief annotated bibliography of materials that we feel may be of special interest to church administrators:

Churchman, C. West. *The Systems Approach.* New York: Dell; Delta Books, 1969.
This book is an attempt to examine what the systems approach means. It does so not from the point of view of selling the idea, but rather examining its validity in a climate of debate.

Drucker, Peter. *Management: Tasks, Responsibilities, Practices.* New York: Harper, 1974.
This is one of the most comprehensive volumes on management available. It is written clearly, crisply, and readably. Every area of management is explored in a very helpful manner. Although written from within a secular and business framework essentially, this book espouses sound basic principles that are usable in moving the church toward its mission. The best one-volume work on the general subject.

————. *The Effective Executive.* New York: Harper, 1967.
Drucker identifies five habits or practices essential to effectiveness. One of the practices is the management of time. Another is choosing what to contribute to the particular organization. A third is knowing where and how to mobilize

strength for best effect. Fourth is setting up the right priorities. And all of them must be knit together by effective decision-making.

Dulles, Avery, S.J. *Models of the Church.* Garden City, N.Y.: Doubleday, 1974.
A comparison of five different models of the church, with an evaluation of each for structuring the church of the future.

Etzioni, Amitai. *Modern Organizations.* Englewood Cliffs, N.J.: Prentice-Hall, 1964.
A study of modern organization theory and structure. Examines organizations as a major aspect of social life. Explicates the impact organizational purposes and structures have upon each other.

Kepner, Charles, and Tregoe, Benjamin. *The Rational Manager: A Systematic Approach to Problem Solving and Decision Making.* New York: McGraw-Hill, 1965.
Develops a step-by-step process for problem analysis and decision analysis. Includes many helpful charts and work sheets. Presents many actual cases to illustrate the use of problem analysis.

Lawrence, Paul, and Lorsch, Jay. *Developing Organizations: Diagnosis and Action.* Reading, Mass.: Addison-Wesley, 1969.
Using concepts from systems analysis, the authors explore three interfaces with reference to organizational development activities. "The criteria we use for determining whether a particular change will lead to the development of the organization at any one or all of these interfaces is whether the change will lead to either a better fit between the organization and the demands of its environment and/or to a better fit between the organization and the needs of individual contributions."

Lindgren, Alvin J. *Foundations for Purposeful Church Administration.* Nashville: Abingdon, 1965.
Seeks to clarify the present confusion as to what church administration is and its place in the church. Its uniqueness is found in its attempt to set forth a philosophy of church administration in a systematic and comprehensive manner.

Odiorne, George. *Management and the Activity Trap.* New York: Harper, 1974.
Discusses the need to clarify the organization's mission and goals as a means of preventing it from drifting into ever increasing, but irrelevant, activity. Especially well written.

Perrow, Charles. *Organizational Analysis: A Sociological View.* Belmont, Cal.: Brooks-Cole, 1970.
Develops a theory and process for analyzing organizational structures, goals, and environment. Based upon the premise that manipulating the organization's structures and analyzing its

goals and environment is a more effective approach to problem-solving than trying to change human behavior.

Rudge, Peter F. *Ministry and Management*. London: Tavistock Publications, 1968.
The aim of this book is to foster the establishment of a theory and a practice of ecclesiastical administration that will stand beside ecclesiastical law and history as an essential part of the corpus of theology and will, furthermore, relate to theories of management as developed in the lay world of business and public administration.

Schein, Edgar H. *Organizational Psychology*. Englewood Cliffs, N.J.: Prentice Hall, 2nd ed., 1972.
The systems-management concept is dealt with very helpfully in this little volume from a psychological perspective. Three separate chapters deal with the process of management, the organization as a complex system, and organizational effectiveness. If you are interested in discovering why organizations—*e.g.*, churches—behave as they do, read this volume. It is sound, helpful, and inexpensive.

Shawchuck, Norman; Worley, Robert C.; Lewis, G. Douglas; and Gray, H. Rhea. *Experiences in Activating Congregations*. Philadelphia: Westminster Press, 1977.
A research report discussing findings on the impact of denominational systems upon the life and development of local congregations, the role of the pastor in developing effective congregational systems, and processes that one project found helpful in activating congregations. A companion volume to *Dry Bones Breathe* by Robert C. Worley.

Worley, Robert C. *A Gathering of Strangers: Understanding the Life of Your Church*. Philadelphia: Westminster Press, 1976.
Provides new perspectives for seeing the church as a functioning institution. Contains exhibits and exercises that will enable church leaders and members to understand the forces that shape their lives in the church. Discusses means by which members with diverse goals, gifts, and expectations can participate in ministry.

———. *Change in the Church: A Source of Hope*. Philadelphia: Westminster Press, 1971.
Brings together theology and the social sciences (especially those concerned with the dynamics of organizations) in order to deal with the problem of change that confronts the church.

———. *Dry Bones Breathe*. Philadelphia: Westminster Press, 1977.
A statement of theological and theoretical understanding of activating congregations based upon the work of Worley, colleagues, and students in hundreds of congregations. It is a fresh insight for leaders on how to think about working toward a

more vital congregation. There are descriptions of processes that leaders can use, with thorough discussion of resources for employing the processes in developing a vital congregation. A companion volume to *Experiences in Activating Congregations* by Norman Shawchuck, *et al.*

A SELECT BIBLIOGRAPHY FOR BUSY PASTORS

We recognize that the above bibliography, though brief in terms of materials currently in print, is nonetheless quite long for a busy pastor. For that reason we have selected a small number of books from the bibliography as perhaps being the most helpful.

Churchman, C. West. *The Systems Approach*.

Drucker, Peter. *Management: Tasks, Responsibilities, Practices*.

Kepner, Charles and Tregoe, Benjamin. *The Rational Manager: A Systematic Approach to Problem Solving and Decision Making*.

Lindgren, Alvin J. *Foundations for Purposeful Church Administration*.

Odiorne, George. *Management and the Activity Trap*.

Shawchuck, Norman, *et al.*, *Experiences in Activating Congregations*.

Worley, Robert C. *A Gathering of Strangers: Understanding the Life of Your Congregation*.

Index

accounting, financial, 95
activity trap, 100
Acts, book of, quoted, 20
administrative board, 78

Bible study group, 51
Body of Christ, the, 26
boundaries, of the system, 50
boundary
  around problem, 110
  defined, 39-40
  as filter, 40, 42
  as monitor, 40
  physical, 39, 40, 42, 43
  sentient, 40, 42-43
brainstorming, 76
budget, 86-87, 89
  worksheet, 98-99
bureaucratic theory. *See* classical
  theory

change, 37, 83
  as cause of problems, 101, 104,
    109, 115
  environmental, 128-29
  safeguard from, 21

  search for, 127
  unavoidable, 129
charismatic leader theory, 22,
  147
charismatic movement, Catholic,
  23
Christ, 14
Christ Church (problem-solving
  case), 102-26
Christian faith, 51
Church, 14, 65
  administration of, 46, 138
  concept of, 51
  history of, 51
  initiating change in, 75-76
  interface with environment,
    65-76
  leaders of, 20-22, 64
  local, 16, 58-59, 101 (*See also*
    local church)
  nature of, 51
  organizational structures in,
    136
  stability of, 74
  structuring of, 67
  wholistic view of, 143
church management, 65

157